NEW PLAINS REVIEW

FALL 2017

I0553436

New Plains Student Publishing
University of Central Oklahoma
Edmond, Oklahoma

Faculty & Staff

EXECUTIVE EDITOR
Shay Rahm

ASSISTANT EXECUTIVE EDITOR
Brendon Yuill

PRODUCTION CHIEF
Michelle Waggoner

WEBMASTER
William Andrews

Editorial Board

EDITOR-IN-CHIEF
Joshua Barnett

PUBLISHING EDITOR
Seth Copeland

MANAGING EDITOR
Anna Doré

SENIOR POETRY EDITOR
Mary Means

SENIOR PROSE EDITORS
Betsy Dickens
Kelsey Smythe

ASSOCIATE EDITORS
Bushra Almogheer
Emily Brooks
Rebekah Brown
Courtney Lockwood-Crull
Kelly McConnell
Trinni Stevens
Alec Whetsel
Zoe Wright
Joseph Zook

Media

PUBLIC RELATIONS DIRECTOR
Andi Ullrich

BLOG EDITOR
Anna Doré

SENIOR DIGITAL EDITOR
Kelsey Smythe

DIGITAL EDITORS
Elizabeth Dickens
Courtney Lockwood-Crull

Design

ART DIRECTOR
Michelle Waggoner

COVER PHOTOGRAPHY
Steven Paul Judd

DIVIDER ART
John Timothy Robinson

NEW PLAINS REVIEW

is a literary journal published each academic semester, sponsored by the English Department, College of Liberal Arts, at the University of Central Oklahoma.

New Plains Logo:
Phantom Warriors (1972),
Sherman Chaddlesone

Web: newplainsreview.com
Email: newplainsreview@gmail.com
twitter: @NewPlainsReview

English Department, Box 184
University of Central Oklahoma
100 North University Drive
Edmond, Oklahoma 73034

Published in USA;
See appendix for printing & manufacturing information.

ISBN-10: 0-9984061-2-0
ISBN-13: 978-0-9984061-2-1

Foreword

THE *NEW PLAINS REVIEW STAFF* WOULD FIRST like to thank the contributors for their amazing prose, plays, poetry, graphic shorts, and visual art. Each new issue has its challenges, but these are always outweighed by its rewards. This year brought the successful release of our new Gender and Sexuality journal, *Central Dissent,* as well as more amazing events. Celebrating Indigenous artists continues to be one of the main focuses of our events and publications. This year's featured speaker for the Sherman Chaddlesone Arts and Letters Lecture Series, Kiowa Choctaw artist Steven Paul Judd, has graciously provided the cover art for this edition. His work is decidedly post-colonial, and challenges the dominant narrative in ways that are both humorous and poignant; his voice fills an ominous hole in our cultural narrative. We would like to thank him for his contributions to New Plains Student Publishing and to the arts.

While *New Plains Review* has a global reach, we are an Oklahoma-based institution. As such, we are excited that our state's current Poet Laureate, Jeanetta Calhoun Mish, contributed "Río de los Carneros Cimarrón" for use as our epigraph. She was born & raised in the heart of the Seminole Nation; she has lived the Oklahoma experience, and continues to codify it with her poetry.

On behalf of the English Department, College of Liberal Arts, University of Central Oklahoma, we are pleased to present to you the Fall 2017 edition of *New Plains Review.*

New Plains Review staff

Río de los Carneros Cimarrón

BY JEANETTA CALHOUN MISH

In Osage country, a river of many names—
Red Fork, Grand Saline, Newsewtonga,
born on a mesa near Folsom, New Mexico
where ancient ones chipped history onto projectile
points, lived amid juniper, ponderosa, and piñon
among brooding volcanoes humped on horizon.

The River of Wild Sheep carves its way
through canyon's gray porphyry palisades,
contests four states' lonely hoodooed borders.

Near Black Mesa where dinosaurs stomped
their feet, where bighorn and antelope graze
shortgrass prairie and bears scratch winter-
weary backs on petrified trees, where shards
of the universe encased in cimmerian silk
glint and glitter, sky-road bright as a turnpike,
the river turns north, hides in its silty channel.

Returning dry and thirsty from its Kansas foray,
the Cimarron southeasts into Oklahoma where
it loans its broad banks to the town of Freedom.

Downstream, its spiced-cider flow drinks from Eagle
Chief and Skeleton Creeks, where few remaining
stands of little bluestem and panic grass reclaim
once-cultivated fields, surrounding ramshackle barns,
singing with the wind in an old prairie dialect,
waving at a pair of bald eagles circling prey.

Below confluence with the Arkansas its wild flow
now dammed into Keystone Lake to host genteel
picnics and regattas—escaping over the weir

El Río promises its stories to the Mississippi.

Contents

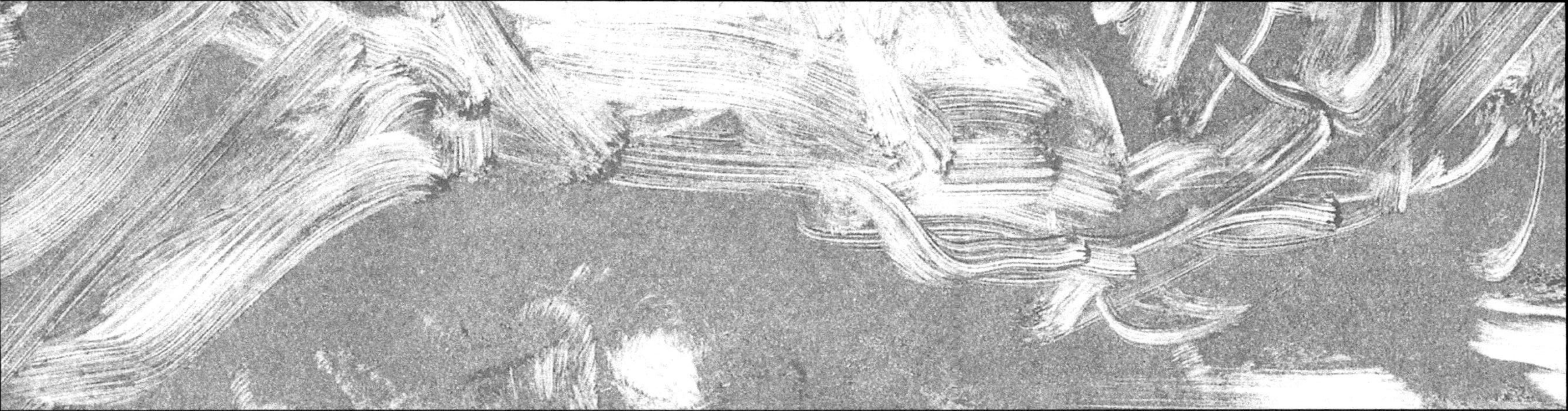

poetry

WAR FACE SEPIA MONOTYPE, 1999

Campground Beach

BY DAVID MIHALYOV

A small boy laughs as wavelets
lick his ankles. Boats rock
on the high tide, sterns
confronting the beach,
as if telling us they don't
have time for youthful frivolity.
They have a higher purpose
if only someone would use them.
Later, when the tide recedes,
they'll rest on wet sand
like toys the boy has abandoned.

Brambles

BY KAREN J. WEYANT

Sitting on the worn path, I sucked
a wounded thumb, watching
my mother wade through thickets
of long, thorny stems. She claimed
the best berries, black as shiny tar

and plump with wild juice, were always
near the top. Thorns pulled her hair,
grabbed at her shirt, but she wore
each prick with a tight smile.
Nearby, catbirds feasted, a chipmunk,

cheeks quivering, scrambled to hide
in the brush. I studied the rotting logs
covered with moss, beer cans
and cigarette butts left over
from a local teen party, then pushed

my finger to my thumb as a single bead
of blood sprang from the spot
where I had reached for ripeness.
Years later, my first boyfriend, wild
with beer, drove his dirt bike through

this same brush while I sat behind him,
clutching his waist, my fingers hooked
around the belt loops of his jeans.
Boots protected my feet, jeans covered
my thighs, yet at home, I still found
scratches where thorns had pricked my skin.

The Summer of Tire Tracks

BY KAREN J. WEYANT

Just north of town, the Johnson boys wore
the fields raw with their three wheelers,
while my Uncle Paul parked his truck
in our garage and then disappeared
with a woman who wasn't my Aunt Fran.
Too young for a real job at Pete's Pizzeria
I watched the Barker twins for less than $3 an hour,
their Big Wheels flying down our front sidewalks
in a rattle of hard plastic and uneven pavement.

For weeks, thick black smoke clouded our streets.
Everyone muttered, The tire heap at R&J's Junkyard,
but no one said the words out loud, just like no one
talked about the Caldwell girls who died
in the two-vehicle collision near Cable Run Road
or how the other driver, beer bottles clicking
in his back seat, walked away, with only a bruise
on his cheek. To get away from the burning rubber,
I bummed a ride to Miller's Pond, wearing
my big sister's swimming suit that sagged
in all the wrong places. Swinging on an old tire
strung high above the stagnant water, hot treads
burned my bare thighs, while miles away, local police,
measured the skid marks left at the crash site,
ignoring the streaks of blood and broken glass.

Contagion

BY PETER SERCHUK

Let us gather it up with a meticulous hand,
scrape it from the unwritten laws of street corners
and statehouses, strip it from the camouflage
of stump speeches and training camps, distill it
from the hallucinations of classrooms and capitals,
mine it from the trap door beneath pulpits
and the illusion of mountain tops.
Yes, let's gather it up from all the mirrors on Earth
and place it here so we can see first-hand how patiently
it waits for reason's end and the heart's collapse.
How it sleeps then wakes, thaws then boils.
How it flows into a reservoir that excites a thirst
so hypnotic and addictive, so easy to excuse
in ourselves that we must drink it, breathe it,
live it and feed it—flirt with it to satisfy
its every whim and plea. No wonder pulses race
in the shadow of its face. It's everything the poets
once thought love could be.

Germination

BY DAVID MIHALYOV

Winter is coming, a long pause.
My daughter worries summer is gone forever.
I explain that although the ground
may freeze, life is underneath, dormant,
waiting for a sign that it's time to begin.
I see her curiosity,
knowing it may take a few years
for the roots to take hold,
before fruit is produced.

What I don't like to ponder
is if today's world is the fruit
from seeds planted years ago.
We search under rocks and fallen
trunks and nothing's to be found.
But what did we expect?
The truth is rarely so visible.
The garden gnome stands guard,
a mocking look that will outlast us all.

Our neighbor sets fire to a caterpillar
nest high in an apple tree.
Hundreds of wriggling, future butterflies
drop, a confused signal to move
wings that don't yet exist.
My daughter watches, curious,
and I wonder who she will become,
what transformations will occur.
But not yet, not yet.

Freed Woman Of Savannah

BY STUART JAMES FORREST

Black gem of Savannah
Her sable woolen hair glistened like wet raven wings,
African rosewood skin
she sold the season's flowers,
long-stemmed red roses, thorns and dry twigs, trimmed.
petals, like deep pools of wine and blood.

Her mamma named her Charm
to keep her child from harm.
She was the town's dear flower girl.
Freed woman of Savannah

The ladies of Savannah
loved her beauty, begrudged her freedom.
Who would not desire to own her.
Black gem of Savannah
Freed woman of Savannah
Whose gentle voice was a caress of the shyest breeze.

African rosewood skin
She was the town's dear flower girl.
Who would not desire to own her,
whose gentile voice was a caress of the shyest breeze.

Noble born of Georgia,
handsome white son of gunpowder and iron,
lover of privilege, women and whiskey,
he saw Charm from his porch,
bid her enter his yard,
seeing her flowers and African rosewood.

His mother named him Caesar
to preordain him a leader
among the town's rich sons.
High born baron of Georgia

Black gem of Savannah
Freed woman of Savannah
Noble born of Georgia
High born baron of Georgia

A rose's freedom is its thorn's sting.
In Savannah, freedom is a fragile thing.
A brandished knife is as strong as a chain
wielded by a noble Georgia baron,
and his threatening knife may do more than merely hurt.
Precious seasonal flowers are destroyed by barren dirt.

Her mamma named her Charm.
His mother named him Caesar.
Freed woman of Savannah
High born baron of Georgia

A sharp-eyed Savannah guardsman found her
beneath bloodstained maple leaves;
a brass button clutched in one cold hand.
A trail of petals may testify when they lead to a door.
A button may bear witness when missing from a shirt
among the town's rich sons.

A trail of wilting petals may reveal a truth
to the wise man who follows
all the way to a high-born son
destined for the gallows.

Pretend
Mountain Region
by Nate Pritts

I pretend that the clouds on the horizon
are mountains because

I need them to be mountains—
      full of anger & resentment
so terrifying & pure—

full of actual rain
& made only out of seething white foam.
I like to pretend

I walked out of my house because you said
it's what you wanted me to do.
      But of course I wanted it too.

There was moonlight in the garden
that I left inside the garden.
      All those coyotes I never saw

loud on the other side of the fence.
In the morning I'd see the grass
crushed down in the places they circled

      obsessive orbits.

All these predawn days trying to escape...

When I remember your face, I pretend
it's a mountain   one I never reached

one that I died on
        frozen & ravaged by the wind.

I start to pretend that the brake lights
of every car out on the highway
are killer stars
        on a mission to burn

the heart right out of me.
But then again
I've always been a little melodramatic.

The worlds that I have found myself in
don't follow any rules I'm aware of.

I need a lot of brand new reasons
not to be afraid.

Guardian

After Rolf Jacobsen

BY TOBI COGSWELL ALFIER

I am the knot
that keeps the sail full and strong.
The compass guiding safe passage
as you turn toward home.

The hand of the angel you turn to,
who reads the braille of your face,
holds you with grace and mercy.

I am the leaves of the trees in winter,
that float in the cool evening breeze.
I kiss your hair, shelter your shoulders
as you walk gently in the shadows.

I am a fleeting image, always fond,
ever near. The way you loved your children
the moment they were born, smooth stones,
or the color blue.

Klans of All Kolors

by Stuart James Forrest

You brawl within a mad house.
You clash within a glass house.
Your violence buries peace
beneath mounds of crystal shards.

When you stand before a colorless God,
what will you boast?
How shall God praise you,
serve you?

Will you be a sovereign people;
a nation within heaven?
Will the beaten, burned, and beheaded rest
as dust beneath your feet?

Come the reckoning and the woe,
and last breaths fade, lost in the wind,
when wit, guile and lies are useless,
and your guns face a wrathful God,

how steady and true will your aim be?

Palimpsests

BY DAVID MIHALYOV

We do the tourist things: blow an Alphorn;
tour a camp; even order wiener schnitzel.
In a postcard village I wonder on whose steps
I walk or if the cobblestone in the square
covers dirt that once absorbed the blood
of public executions.

An elderly gentleman is helped onto a bench
by a boy too young to ask about the past.
As they feed birds I wonder if he shot
at my father in the war, another scared youth.
The man laughs at something the boy says
so I force my questioning to recede.

At dinner we share a long table with a group
of locals keeping time with empty wine bottles.
They don't speak English and we don't
sprechen much Deutsch. I look at their happy
faces. Some of their grandparents
must have been complicit, and I wonder if

farther back, my antecedents took part
in the pogroms of their day, if
our lives conceal their sins. It's too much
or me, on vacation, to judge, so, today,
I forgive our forebears, forgive the old man,
and offer a silent toast to everyone's ghosts.

The Sailing Stones

BY TIM ROLANDS

Rocks here dream of distant hills.

When the world at night turns to sleep
they uncurl and stretch stiff joints,

cracking echoes across the valley.

When rain falling late into the night
floods and flashes ice on the flats,

they rise and conspire together
to leave the valley forever,

to walk among faraway hills,
taste the spray of lonely seas,

plunge into swaying waves—
the salt an unexpected memory,

the descent through fathoms of cold
and dark an unwanted nightmare

with glimpses of an unlit city
ever further below,

its walls and twisted towers
marshaling the black end of night.

They wake on cracked earth
beneath a wide empty sky,

sky enough to swallow oceans whole.

Rules of Chess

BY PETER SERCHUK

The Pawn is always a pawn, a sucker the dealer spots
a mile away, a collector of dreams with pockets full of holes.
Year after year, he's ready to follow whichever King tells
the best lie. He walks behind the royal mount with a shovel,
digs the royal moat, builds the royal castle and sooner
or later volunteers his final breaths for not-so-royal wars,
killing nameless pawns of other colors.

The Rook knows that he's an outcast, relegated to corners,
shuffling side to side. By living on the edge, he's learned
that pride is deadly. Better to be quick and nimble outside
the line of fire. Better to be half as tall as the living and twice
as smart as the dead. He's too far from the King to envy
his crown. When the sky begins to fall, when the clock is
winding down, he knows it's best to stay close to the Queen
for she is the Pièce de Résistance.

The Knight and his steed are one, indistinguishable
even to their spouses. Both are brave but the horse is wiser,
charging ahead toward the point of a lance, then a quick step
sideways. To see them in full regalia, one couldn't guess
they once earned their stripes in the circus; chasing after
lazy clowns and jumping through hoops of fire. Until that
fateful day when they were drafted to trade the laughter
of children for the tantrums of the Sire.

The Bishop stands straight and tall, so close to both King
and Queen he imagines himself of royal blood. No fool for
the afterlife, he knows this is where the real game is played;
so his faith is flattering the upper hand just in case heaven
doesn't return his calls. Still, being the Creator's ambassador
on Earth, naturally he prays for peace, love and a better world.
But until that day comes, his path is traveling the diamond's edge,
ready to surprise non-believers with the light of darkness.

Everyone is devoted to their Queen, especially the King,
for love may follow the wind but only devotion saves you
from the grave. Her music is the drumbeat of the hour.
As she moves, so moves the Kingdom and she moves
whichever way desire or necessity demands.
God save the Queen! God save the Queen!
If she lives to old age, victory is assured. And if she dies
young, *then things fall apart, the center cannot hold,*
as one wise Irish bard once foretold.

The King keeps himself hidden, miles behind the front lines
of chance. His crown aside, he's powerless. He sits on a throne
of other men's blood surrounded by mirrors. The mirrors
are clean but his eyes are not, so what he sees reflected is
always twice the size of any doubt. All through the battle,
he shuffles back and forth, front and back, paralyzed by fear,
begging the Knight to stand beside him, the Bishop to repeat
how God adores him, the Rook to stand watch on the parapet
and the Queen to love him, for all he is and cannot be,
until the bitter end.

The Blind Woman Dictates a Poem to Her Love

BY TOBI COGSWELL ALFIER

I used to know how you looked:
strong arms, wrists like a deckhand
on trawlers, your nets reaping tons
from the sea. Arms that could go ten
rounds with anyone in the ring—
you still have the belts and trophies.

The back of your neck dark red
from the sun. No hat could protect you,
only a hooded parka in snow, when your thighs
became tough as telephone poles
in Texas, relentless and intense
against twisters and hail.

The white of your covered and protected
torso. Narrow-waisted, ribbed from sit-ups
you do each night, the arrow of light brown
hair guiding me to another place I love,
the fiery part of you—the reason I learned
to always leave the lights on with you.

And your kind face. No words to describe
the ruddy intelligence brooding
behind thoughtful eyes the color of seaglass,
if collected from glaciers, white-blue and bold
as they showed without doubt how much
I was loved, no matter the amount we debated.

I can still hear your sit-ups, your counts as they
get short of breath and then breathless. Of course
I can feel your arms around me, hear your whispers
stroke my many insecurities. But the lights—absent
as color on a moonless night. How frost hides
the beauty of a mountain stream, so much is lost.

Flowers Planted During an Eclipse Will Bloom More Brightly

BY C. WADE BENTLEY

It's not like the old days. During the coming
total eclipse, very few virgins will be offered
up to the Sun God. Only a relatively small
number of secluded fundamentalists in Idaho
will prostrate themselves upon the ground, lo,
in fear and trembling. Thanks to the new god

Google, there won't be enough people who believe
witches are to blame to even assemble a proper,
self-righteous, pitchfork-and-torch mob
to march on the home of the local uppity
poetess. Precious few wide-eyed innocents

will stare so long at the sky they mistake
a seared retina for a dog or frog or dragon
noshing on our medium-sized yellow dwarf star.
Oh, there are still a few holdouts who hold

that eclipses pose a danger to the unborn, but where,
I ask you, are your YouTube public service
announcements, your telethons, your Kickstarters?

Let's face it, a caravan of campers in Wyoming

throwing back a case of Coors is but a pale
imitation, another excuse to flood Facebook
with videos, all captioned, "So cool—it was light,
and then it got really dark, and then it got light
again." No one will return to his job crunching
numbers at Goldman Sachs cut to the quick,
quickened with renewed gratitude that a fall harvest

will still happen, that the gods have seen fit
to tolerate him a while longer. I mean, if the day
becoming as night, the sudden disappearance
of the source of all that is warm and good,
the realization, after a lifetime of self-absorption,

that we are but a pretty rock, held by the grace
of gravity in the halo of a beneficent and, apparently,
tenuous hydrogen bomb—if this isn't enough
to cause naked heathens to erupt into a flash mob
dance-off in my suburban cul-de-sac, what hell
is this world coming to?

Questions to a Male Praying Mantis

BY PETER HOGAN

Hey buddy, do you know
what you got yourself into? Gods, legends,
men scraped across night sky. What happens

when you give part of yourself
you can't get back? Do you learn? Realize
she only does this when she's hungry?

How close is a bite to a kiss?
Was it raining? Did you forget
that all foreplay is hypnotic? Waltz

and swirls. Swirls and waltz and swirls.
And you're there, lighting a post sex cigarette.
Are diamond rings made for pincers? Tiny homes

with toothpick fences? Did you take her
to meet your parents? What would you
have named the child? Do you have to

watch? Is she courteous? Begins with
the eyes? When her lips purse, do you see
fangs? Or are you already a man

with a taut bow? A pointed arrow. Kaleidoscope.
Swirls of tiny lights in empty,
unnamed spaces. Her. So it doesn't matter

how much she takes. Is this the end goal?
Buddy, is this better
than being alone? Or is it the same?

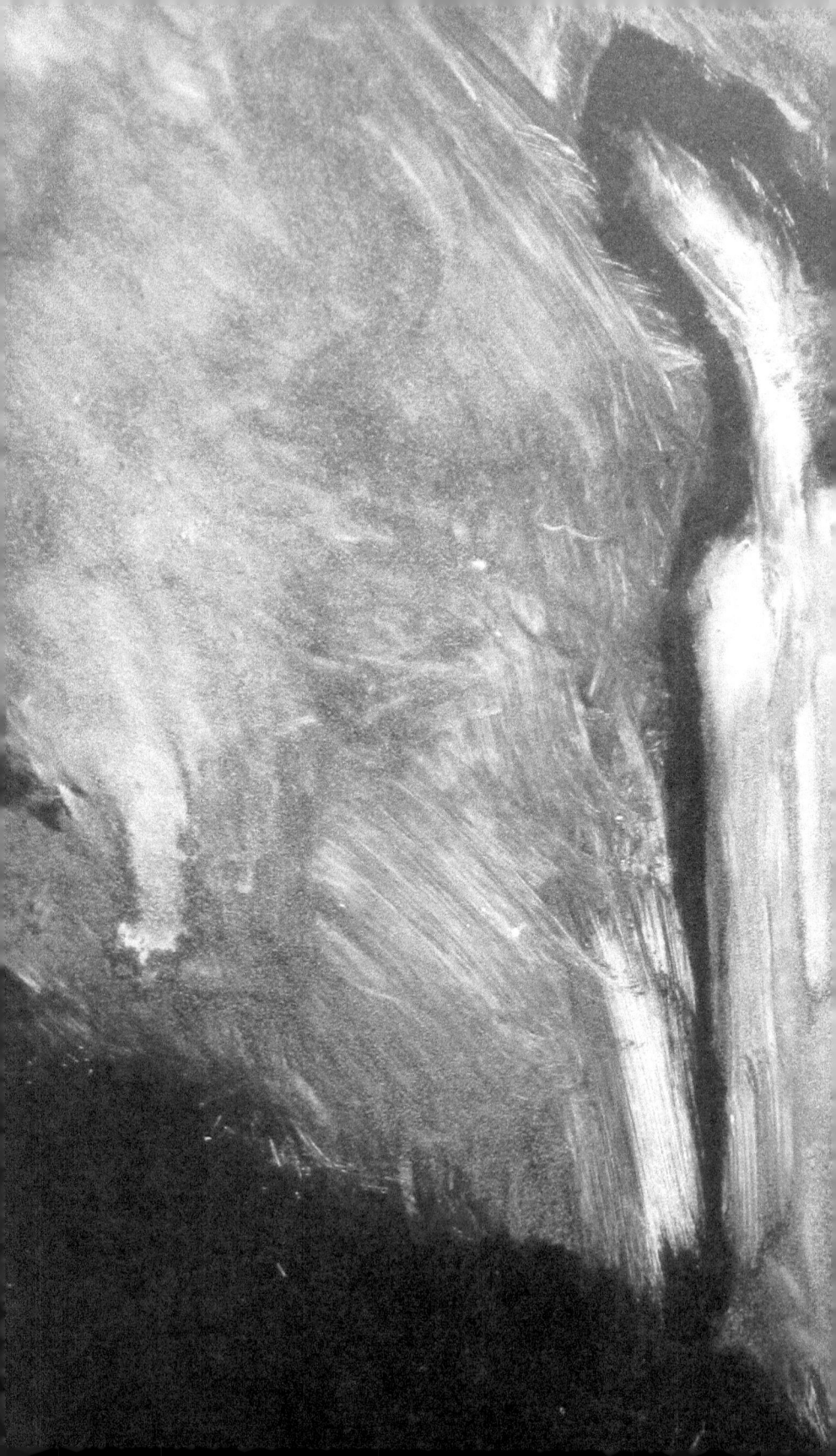

sherman chaddlesone
flash fiction contest

CANDLE MONOTYPE, 1999

*B*ORN ON JUNE 2, 1947, SHERMAN CHADDLESONE is recognized as a world renowned Kiowan artist, teacher, veteran, and general promoter of the arts. Originating from Oklahoma, Chaddlesone created such pieces as "A Silent Thunder in My Heart," and "Following the Ragweed Sundance" throughout his career. After returning to Oklahoma from his travels across both the United States and the globe, Chaddlesone studied at the University of Central Oklahoma as he began to shift his artistry into a full-time career, during which time he created "Phantom Warriors," which New Plains Review has based its logo on with his permission.

To commemorate the life and works of Sherman Chaddlesone, *New Plains Review* created the Sherman Chaddlesone Flash Fiction Contest. The contest attracted over a hundred and fifty submissions from writers across the globe, and was judged by the staff of New Plains Student Publishing before being finally judged by Dr. Constance Squires.

With this, we congratulate the winner of this contest, Bart Everson, for his piece "Kerry was in the Kitchen, Cooking." His piece will be accompanied by the other finalists in the Fall 2017 edition of the *New Plains Review.*

WINNER OF THE SHERMAN CHADDLESONE FLASH FICTION CONTEST

Kerry Was in the Kitchen, Cooking

BY BART EVERSON

KERRY WAS IN THE KITCHEN, COOKING. MARCUS would be home soon, and she wanted to have dinner ready. She had chosen a recipe, bought the ingredients, and even set the table already, with a little vase of yellow flowers in the center. But perhaps she had spent a little too much time on the preparations. It was 5:15 now, and the casserole wasn't even in the oven yet. Marcus was probably halfway down I-35 by this time. But Kerry was afraid to rush, afraid she might measure something wrong or leave out some key ingredient. Then the whole meal would be ruined, and Marcus would be disappointed. But if dinner wasn't ready when Marcus came home then he would be very angry. Kerry wondered which would be worse. Marcus was bound to be hungry; he'd been away all day working so hard. So perhaps it would be best to rush ahead and risk making a mistake. But on the other hand, Marcus had a strong sense for what was proper—he hated sloppiness—and he always said that he wanted a wife who could cook like his mother had.

The panes of glass rattled in the window frame, startling Kerry so much that she dropped the mixing bowl. Was that his car pulling into the garage? No, just the garbage men coming around again. How long had she been standing there lost in thought? The casserole ought to have been done by now. She looked down at the mess on the floor, a spreading puddle of greasy gray. This meant starting over from scratch.

Kerry knelt and started wiping the puddle up. In no time at all her dishrag was soaked with the stuff and wouldn't take anymore. She continued scrubbing across the tiles for awhile, but it only splashed the mess around. Eventually she gave up and tried to rinse the cloth out in the sink. But the grease had caked, and the cloth would not come clean. It was ruined.

She threw the dishrag into the garbage bag and looked for something more absorbent. But she couldn't find a sponge or towel anywhere. Her eyes fell on the tablecloth. It would take several minutes of her precious time to remove the place settings and then put them back, but she had no choice. She couldn't just leave the mess on the floor.

When she had gotten the tablecloth off and knelt down once again, however, she realized that it was actually made of plastic, and it wouldn't absorb any of the spilt ingredients. How could she have failed to notice?

It was 5:45. Marcus was late, thank God, although there was little chance now of making things right. She left the tablecloth spread over the mess and ran to the refrigerator. She would have to heat up some leftovers; there was simply no other choice. She hated to think what Marcus would say about leftovers, but what else could she do?

A carton of milk, eggs, jelly, cottage cheese... Where were the leftovers? Kerry searched each shelf, but she couldn't find any. Perhaps she had forgotten what they looked like. They would be in Tupperware, yes, little white plastic containers. More of an off-white, really. With transparent lids. "Now let's see," she murmured, sucking the tips of her fingers. She had a whole army of Tupperware containers—about twenty in all, far more than she could ever possibly use. Half of them were round and the other half were square. She preferred the square ones because it seemed to her that they would be more efficient for storing food if the refrigerator was crowded, and she clearly remembered making a decision to use the square containers first, and to use the round containers only when all the square ones were full. There were bound to be lots of leftovers because Kerry liked to cook large meals; that's what Marcus' mother had done, after all. Kerry used the leftovers as quick lunches for herself while Marcus was away at work. It would never do to serve him leftovers for dinner. But tonight Kerry had been reduced to that, only there didn't seem to be any leftovers in the refrigerator.

It was very odd. Kerry shut the refrigerator door and looked at the clock. 6:00! Marcus should have been home a long time ago. Kerry never once imagined that her husband had gotten held up at the office. He was too efficient for that; he always got his work done well ahead of time. Nor did she think that he might have gotten stuck in a traffic jam. He was an excellent driver, and his car was so fast and powerful that he never got caught in traffic. And it never entered Kerry's mind that he might have been involved in an accident. Marcus was too careful for that; he always thought ahead and planned the safest route home, and besides that, his eyesight was keen and reflexes were as quick as lightning.

Kerry threw opened the cabinet doors. "Ah-ha!" There was the Tupperware, all of it. Twenty pieces, just as she'd said. She counted to make sure. Yes, ten square and ten round, all of them off-white, gleaming, perfectly clean. Price stickers still affixed. Brand new. Never used. Kerry thought there was something strange about the way they caught the light, something almost sinister. How long had they been sitting there in the dark cabinet together? The rows of blank plastic shapes stared out at her like the blind eyes of a cavefish, as if they couldn't see anything. They were gleaming unnaturally bright; in fact, they seemed to be swelling like giant mushrooms. Kerry stumbled back and clutched at a kitchen knife.

Then the panes of glass rattled in the window frame again, and Kerry knew that it really was Marcus this time, pulling his car into the garage. The whole house was shaking. She heard the motor die; the door flew open and slammed shut again, and then he was there in the kitchen.

"Hi, honey. I'm home."

Kerry dropped the knife into the sink. She hardly dared look up at him. Absently she noted that she was standing in a pool of gray grease. What would Marcus say? What would he do?

He touched her chin, lifted her head. He was smiling sadly. In his other hand he held a white paper sack.

"Chinese today," he said, lifting the sack. "Are you hungry?"

Firefly

BY JULIE GARCÉS

*I*COULD'VE SWORN ONE OF MY MOTHER'S IMPORTANT
court papers had just flown out the window as we sped
down the dark turnpike, the illuminated needle of the
odometer creeping near 90 on the Oldsmobile's dashboard,
my brother and I in the back seat as Mom cranked up "I Just
Called to Say I Love You," by Stevie Wonder, her cigarette
tip a flickering red cherry in the night. We hated when she
smoked and usually made overt displays of coughing and
choking that would rival the finales of some high school
renditions of a Shakespearian tragedy. But at the end of
this day we turned to look at each other and I could see
a tiny bit of fright in my brother's eyes. He was seven and
I was nine.

Mom had been running late for a court date that morning as she drove us to school. But on a whim, that was not
entirely whimsical given her personality, she announced,
"Road trip!" and made a wide u-turn in the opposite direction,
the tires crunching then spitting the rocks on the side of
the road as if making a mess of breakfast cereal. She pulled
into a 7-11 and let us buy all the candy and potato chips we
wanted. Even slurpees.

As we sat in the back seat with no idea where we were
headed, my stomach ached in a torrid swirl. The day's sugar
rush plunged me into a lethargic sleepiness. It was a custody
battle she was avoiding, so bitter no one was left unsullied
in the mud-strewn courtroom. Our father claimed Mom was
unpredictable and lacking structure for us. While Dad was
frugal with his money and debated over every new toy, pair
of shoes, or afterschool activity, Mom spoiled us with state

of the art roller skates, expensive dinners at steak houses, and enough new clothes to overstuff the closets. Things we didn't even want. She picked me up from school one day with a brand new trumpet so shiny I could see the look of bewilderment on my face in its polished brass. I had no idea how to play it and the case sat collecting dust in the corner of my room.

And so Mom had spent every penny Dad had budgeted for her and was broke by Monday so we had to eat PB&J sandwiches until Friday. But even now, this hi-jacking of us had lasted much longer than any of the times she took us to The Keys or to the water park in Tampa. Disneyworld crossed my mind. Maybe she would buy us new clothes and mouse ears while we were there.

I held my breath and tried not to inhale the smoke filled air. She flicked the last of the cigarette out the window.

"That's littering," I pointed out, but she kept singing and smiling, now digging around the console for her to-go coffee.

The exit for Disneyworld came and went. I pointed it out to my brother and waved to it as we drove past. Every time we had asked Mom where we were going she said "you'll see" or "it's a surprise" and turned the music up louder. So now we couldn't even hear each other and only made hand gestures. My brother turned in his booster seat, forlorn, and sank his chin into his chest.

Finally we pulled off the turnpike, made some turns then headed down a dark stretch of road. We had made stops earlier in the day, where Mom had alternated between laying on a picnic table in the sun, jacking up her tank top and shorts for maximum sun exposure, and searching nearby marshes to add to her collection of cat tails, dead butterflies and beetles "for an art project," she claimed.

We passed a sign that read, "Now entering Lake Griffin State Park" and then another that read "Dead River" with an arrow pointing the way ahead. I reached for my brother's hand and shivered as the headlights cut through a low mist. My mother turned the radio off and the sound of frogs and crickets filled the air as she lowered the windows. She parked and got out. We followed.

"I want to show you two something very special," she said as she took both of our hands. We walked down a nature trail, under a hammock of leaning oak trees. The path opened up to a meadow next to the river. A marshy, decaying stink hung in the air. In the distance, we could see the reason for the drive. She let our hands go and ran ahead. The moon gave us just enough light to follow her.

We ran too and then, as if being in the center of a hurricane, we were surrounded by thousands of lightning bugs. They glowed like stars twinkling in the sky. Some flickered fast, some slow and some not at all. We laughed as they swarmed around us, sometimes crashing against us in their frenzy, falling, then slowly flying up again.

I looked at my brother and he was grinning a wide electric smile. A lightning bug had smashed itself into his mouth and its gooey luminescence was smeared across his teeth, making them glow like the Cheshire Cat's. Seconds later, he spit out a long trail of saliva and whined about a taste worse than expired Nyquil.

"No matter what anyone ever says," she told us, "I wanted to show you myself. This is how much I love you." She held her arms wide as the bugs floated around us, streaking blue trails. "More than all the fireflies, more than all the stars in the universe." And when we looked up there were more stars than we had ever seen, held together by a milky cobweb in the dark sky.

She kissed us both on our foreheads on that humid, buggy night and even years later, when we had thought she lost her mind, in the midst of delirium, when all she could do was cry or be silent she would whisper, "remember the fireflies."

We never told Dad where we went that day. Mom called him the morning after and only said she needed some quality time. The court granted him full custody with visitation for our mother on the weekends. This probably worked out for the best because Father got us to bed early and to school on time, boring as it was.

When I was a teenager, I took some friends to the same spot at Lake Griffin. We staggered down the path, drunk and passing around blunts big enough to choke an alligator. There were no fireflies there that night or any other night I returned.

Occasionally I'll see one or two float past me as I stand in my backyard, barefoot in the wet grass on a balmy summer night. I'll think about how the world will never understand that some people have hearts ever expanding in this cold, black universe. That some people need the freedom to make light where there is nothing but darkness.

Real Beaut

BY KALYN MCALISTER

F IRST YEAR OF GRADUATE SCHOOL, SIXTH YEAR at the same university, twelve years out from a twelve-year lower education, half that long since leaving the service, four years into an unrequited love, and five since I'd last felt it. I had come home to the heartland, that place of mercurial weather and women. She sat behind me the first day of class. It was the beginning of love.

When I first saw her hair, falling from crown to hips, strands at her lips, I was smitten. My old bad habit fired up again. Every day, I looked forward to a glimpse of her as she walked in front of me to her seat in the back of the room, shimmering pyre flickering against her back.

I moved so I could be near her. She eyed me up and down for the first time as I sat, motioning as I did as if to ask her permission. Eyes narrowed, she shrugged. But a small smile plied at the corner of her lips where a wild strand of hair teased. She brushed it away.

I looked away and saw the classroom, like every other, like my high school's.

The day I turned sixteen, when school let out, I saw my dad in the parking lot next to a shiny new truck. My older sisters gave me hell for it. Dad hadn't been around when they turned sixteen, and they accused me of being his favorite. But they would only sell it and give the money to their deadbeat boyfriends or their diligent dealers.

I took my high school crush on the inaugural drive. That love lasted four years too. The beginning of my bad habit, maybe. It was a warm day for February, so we drove with the windows down. She brushed the hair away from her mouth, where it danced wildly as if as entranced as I was.

Now, looking at the classroom, I remembered that other school, and the senior prom I missed. My crush had asked me to skip it, hang out instead, too cool for school dances. And the look on my date's face the next day, when she came to my house, May wind whipping her tight ponytail that kept it out of her face. She had tears in her eyes and asked "Why?"

"A bad habit," I had responded.

I couldn't look at her then. She reminded me of my mom asking me why—my father would leave us. Of my sisters' bitterness at his present to me when he resurfaced years later with a new woman. Not new. We knew her. That was the beginning of my bad habit.

I turned to the girl beside me, hair covering half her face. "Had to get out of the front row. Terrible first-day seating mistake."

I felt the first flush of enchantment. I wanted to take her on a drive in the truck I no longer had, back to the old classrooms, back to my dad waiting for me in the parking lot.

She forced a tiny smile. Politely. There was a pause. "You never know, sitting next to me could be your worst mistake." She spoke like a flame.

Tachypsychia

BY JOSH SHEPARD

*A*S THE CONCRETE RISES TO MEET YOUR BODY, you are struck with the thought of how falling really doesn't feel like falling at all. It is a moment, nearly frozen, but slowly thawing, almost imperceptibly even now. A moment of hypersensitivity. Heightened awareness. *How strange.* How easily you can pinpoint every little sensation, each nuance.

You feel everything.

As the blood-warmth spreads from the epicenter below your left eye across the rest of your cheek, a second fist finds refuge square in your solar plexus. It doesn't feel anything like people say it does. Where did the phrase "the wind knocked out of you" come from? That's not what this feels like. No. It feels . . . exactly like it is. You feel your diaphragm spasm and lock up—complete paralysis. And that's the thing: the problem isn't so much the air rushing out; it's your inability to draw another breath in.

Is this what drowning feels like?

Doubled over, you gasp, deep, as your body remembers how to breathe. That's when the right-cross lands on your jaw. You see a bright flash of white, then everything fades in with flashing lights, celestial snow. *Seeing stars.* You open your mouth, wide, and it hurts. You understand that your jaw is dislocated. More static comes in as your mouth is closed for you with an uppercut from another fist, a perfect floating assailant.

That's when you taste it.

The unmistakeable metallic cocktail of a mouthful of blood. Strange how blood has such a sharp taste with it being mostly water and barely any iron at all really. You chalk it up to the sheer acuteness of the human senses. It's the same way one might smell a trace amount of sulfur in the air, the rotten egg scent of carbon monoxide. It's a survival instinct at its core.

You find yourself analyzing the taste the way a true connoisseur might with wine. Instead of notes of blackberry or hints of rose it's a touch of nickel, and . . . is that copper maybe? No, cobalt. Columns of metals on the periodic table flash before you, then the image of a stemmed glass full of loose change. You're, of course, aware of the absurdity of it all; after all, you know about hemoglobin and red blood cells and the gustatory system.

You feel electric fire shoot from the nerve between your Adam's apple and chin through the rest of your body. The moment lasts an eternity.

Then finally the ground comes crashing back up at you.

You lie on the ground staring upward, wondering which stars are real and which one's aren't. You wonder if it matters either way.

And you feel nothing.

Submerged

by Megan Thomson Connor

April 5th

Dearly Beloved,

I am writing to you from the bottom of the garden pond. Here, rooted in the dark, it is as if I am in the underworld, in the belly of the earth. I feel close to you here. The weight of the water wraps itself around my shoulders. When I look up, I can see the afternoon sunlight filtering through the algae and lily pads. I blow bubbles and the Koi that survived the winter dart among them.

After your death in November, the children looked to me for comfort. It was the first time I ever felt needed. But as the Spring thaws, they appear to be hardening into their former selves as though you are still here.

Eli is a monstrous height although you wouldn't know it as he spends most of his time curled over, fern-like. He loves all things electric. He rarely speaks and his right thumb scrolls through everything so fast. He will never understand what it is like to sit at the bottom of a pond while his children turn into strangers.

Victoria is an enigma. I only know her through the mountains of clothing on her bedroom floor. They recede and then erupt corresponding with the shifting plates of high school. Sometimes, I catch her at the breakfast table and I long to reach out and stroke her static curls but I don't. If she senses my want, she ignores it.

I digress. The dusk has seeped into the world without my noticing. My own handwriting is almost illegible and my fingers resemble dried-figs. Sleep sweet.

Yours truly,
Jonathan

May 11th

Dearly Beloved,

I left my last letter for you on your dresser. I hope you got it. I am sorry if it was still damp. As I tucked myself into bed that night, I wondered if you do in fact sleep. Does the bitter taste of night reach your mouth? I write to you again from the bottom of the pond but I think you already knew that. I sense your presence in the weeds' lazy tendrils, the ripples on the surface, the sway around me.

Victoria came home at two last night. Although she had broken her curfew, she did not walk with care. She slammed doors and ran the shower. I told myself that she is reaching out in her disobedience. Yet, I know this is false. She does not hate or pity me. When I try to reach out to her, I am not met with hostility. I am met with indifference. It is a much crueler fate. I do not exist, just as I did not exist before.

I wish I could experience what Victoria and Eli feel. See the world through their eyes, although I fear what I would find. I remember one winter when we stood under the golden glow of a lamppost in the snow. It was so quiet and the world turned slower that night. We watched the light catch every snowflake as if filled with some human hunger for nostalgia. The sepia reel plays in my head, sickly and sweet. Do our children have those moments? Does time ever slow down for them? Do they know about the unsolvable pain of childhood? The eternal losses there are to mourn?

Is it strange for a father to wish his children to feel pain? I admit, I sometimes do, even if it is just the tiniest amount.

Yours truly,
Jonathan

Dearly Beloved,

I am taunted by the empty shells of our children. Where did their substance go? I want to shake them awake, hit them hard, make them feel something.

I am not a bad man, but here in the curve of the pond, my darkest thoughts float to the surface of my mind. I try to push them down so I will not scare you but they are buoyant and bounce back with more force. Some of your Koi have died. Their tiny skeletons scrape the floor like fingernail clippings.

I imagine where you are to be like the 1950s. Women wear full skirts and red lipstick. Children respect their fathers and we sleep in four-poster beds. Life is simple. The only thing that is complex is the beauty in the nature around us. Our children play with skipping ropes and chalk. Technology has not advanced in my paradise.

One day we will all be there together. Free from this chaotic and disorderly life that dulls the senses.

Yours truly,
Johnathan

May 23rd

Dearly Beloved,

Yesterday, the strangest thing happened. I emerged from the water just as the heavens flushed pink. Eli was sitting on the skeleton of a climbing frame he loved as a child. The neighbor's lawn mower hummed its last row and the sound of crickets stirred the air. He held up his phone to take a picture of the clouds and as he lowered it, a miracle occurred. His head remained raised towards the sky. I felt as though I were in a dream. He did not see me ankle deep in the reeds, water dripping off my tie.

Back in the house, he returned to the blue light of his computer screen, but the joy of the sunset stayed with me. All I have ever wanted is a moment for our children to succumb to the beauty of this world. I saw Eli's inhalation as a swollen sun set the clouds on fire. I imagined Victoria, out with her friends, watching the sky break golden at the fold of the horizon. I do not know what changed in Eli that evening or if it will ever happen again but I fell asleep still wearing a smile. I cannot express to you how elated I feel.

Yours truly,
Jonathan

June 1st

Dearly Beloved,

I am embarrassed at the naiveté of my last letter. It should have been obvious to me. For her birthday, Victoria placed blankets on the lawn and had a picnic with her friends. They lazed in the grass for hours with berry-red smiles. I know that you were the one who raised Eli's chin to the sky and lured Victoria out of the house with a gentle warm wind. I don't know whom you've befriended in the underworld but you were always resourceful.

The ink on my paper has already begun to run. It gathers vein-like from the corners of words. Black streams pool into one another. It is no matter, I know that my words will reach you in the dark. Was it my fantasies of our family in the underworld that forced your interference? A mother's love can do wonders when you threaten her young. Did you think I'd kill them too? Were you afraid I'd follow?

Nothing will stop me from joining you, Marcy. You can't run out the clock. We will be together again. Every day the air chips away at my skin and the lines on my hands gather like city maps. My heart warms to think of you in the next life. I see you hip-deep in children with a Hollywood smile and soft hands. My jaw is straight and strong, my presence commands attention. You need me more than I need you.

I lie on my back and feel the weight of the water on my beating chest. I am in no hurry. Besides me, in the mud, lies your softened self. It has eroded some since my last letter.

Yours truly,
Jonathan

Gespo the Mannequin

BY ROSS WHITE

Over there, yonder—he's set on the mantelpiece,
now, a jagged silhouette with the low light—

merely cylinders of oak, strung together with wire—
a painted doll, amateur in its creation, savage in its
crude appearance. Still, the wooden hands
seemed to have been made so painstakingly—
a type of obsessive love was poured into it.

Sleep well, for the black eyes of the mannequin
can see after the snuffing of the candlelight.

Sleep well, youngster. The carefully built pile of
toenails and fingernails in your closet is but a temple,
a shrine to keep the slippery things at bay—
though you never hear his collections, the geriatric
struggles of wood and wire on the move.

Wild lanky wires make up his hair, sprouting in
all directions from the flat top of his head, the
dance of those in the still night mesmerize the
sleepless into dreams. Sleep well, he needs not the
dreams; the little beetles that his red-dyed cloth
heart has embraced dream his dreams for him.
Voiceless is his language; scattered are his ideals.

Sleep. Sleep, forget that when I wrap my body
around your bodies, I wrap around your necks
with so many black wires and splintered fingers.
sleep doesn't come to me, doesn't come for me.

Wait patiently for the bulbous clouds to trundle over;
   lightless wind is his friend— so many friends, the
tumid raccoon beneath the house, scratching of naked
   branches on the foggy window, comforting silence
in the aftermath of weeping, the little brown beetles
   that crawl from resting places—truncated minds,
   squalid brains— sleeps well, among Gespo's gaze.

Painted across his middle are the runes of the
   chewed children, a spattering of strange symbols,
once upon a time white and bright—quite the sight—
   turned mildewed yellow and brown, seeping
      down into the rotted cracks of carved oak.

Whispers? It's the tread of memories along the
wet carpet of the living, there are so many things
   to whisper about. Slithering under the covers,
      he feels for fright and finds. Always finds.

His snickering signals the absence of the wakeful,
only heard by one, a chittering that stutters and
gasps with high-pitched squeaks, the noise of a child
under the wires. Sleep well, these are no concerns
for ones who drift from reality in the night.

The minutes tick slowly, every second scored in the
quiet of the greasy oak, an endless counting and
fleeting pondering. Reasons have no meaning inside
the twisted wires, dreams have no meaning but to flee
from forever, yellowed painted symbols resemble a
visage with a gaping mouth—machinery's disregard
for the cultured coterie that we keep. Lost in the
passing of time, the hands that carved him to be.

Fluff your baby blue blankets and pull them
past your neck, nothing to worry about, worry about the
nothing, the nothing in the dark corner of the room.
A fake thing can't do much harm. Sleep well, youngster.

Scissors

BY MATTIE LEE ELLIOTT

FIRST, SHE NEEDED DIFFERENT SCISSORS. THE pink-handled school scissors with the rounded tip would not work. Chris went to the kitchen and took the orange-handled scissors from the junk drawer. They were almost as long as her arm, and they were viciously pointed. She ran her finger down one blade and then the other, shivering at the razor sharpness. Perfect. She took the scissors back to her bedroom and shut the door.

In the top dresser drawer there were twelve pairs of clean, white underwear—two packs of seven, minus one in the hamper and one that was gone. Chris stacked them neatly on the floor and sat down beside them with her back against the door. She picked up the first pair and carefully examined the pink satin bow on the waistband. She held the bow tightly in her left hand, the scissors in her right, and focused on the tiny pink threads, careful not to cut the elastic. Snip. She exhaled, sat up straight, and squared her shoulders.

Soon Chris had a mound of little pink bows and a pile of plain white underwear. It wasn't enough, not yet. Her chest still felt tight, and there was a dull, persistent ache at the base of her skull.

Chris took all the jeans from her closet. It was the first week of school, and her jeans still smelled like dye. She took each pair methodically off its hanger. One, two, three, four, five, six. Six pairs of jeans, size Six-X. She stuffed a pair of underwear into each pant leg. Perfect. Chris opened the bedroom door and walked to the laundry room, her arms full of clothes, her nose full of the smell of new denim.

Standing on her stool in front of the washing machine, Chris poured detergent carefully up to the fill line in the cap. She turned the knobs. Cold water, regular cycle, start. She walked back down the hall, listening to her bare feet slap-slapping against the tiles. She could feel the floor under her feet again; she wasn't floating. She stood still for a minute, studying her toes, before returning to her room.

Chris opened her treasure box and took out an empty pill bottle. She push-twist-opened the childproof cap. She gathered the bows from the floor and squeezed them tightly in her left hand before stuffing them into the pill bottle and putting the lid back on. She put the bottle in the back corner of her closet, behind the toy box.

The scissors lay on the carpet, their sharp beak begging for work. Chris unbraided her hair, the left pigtail, then the right. She sat on the edge of the bed for a long time, holding the scissors and not thinking anything. She sighed. Good little girls don't cut their hair.

After putting the scissors back in the kitchen drawer, Chris put her laundry into the dryer. Signal on, medium heat, more dry, start. She stood for forty-five minutes, staring at the dryer, listening to the rhythmic clang of buttons against the metal drum. What was it like in there, being tossed over and over and around and around, hitting the walls at every turn?

The sound of the buzzer made her jump. She carefully hung up six warm pairs of Six-X jeans and neatly folded twelve pairs of powder blue underwear. Putting away the clean clothes, she noticed one pink, satin bow on the floor in front of the dresser. She picked it up and held it gently, like she was holding a butterfly.

Chris sat down on the lid of the toy box in the closet. She pulled the door shut, pressed the little pink bow to her chest, and allowed herself to cry. She cried until the tightness and the ache were gone, and she was empty, like a locust shell. She took a breath and opened the closet door. She brushed her long hair back into a low ponytail and washed her face. She looked in the bathroom mirror. She still looked like a good little girl.

"Good little girls make me sick."

Her reflection nodded in agreement.

Chris put her last pink bow into her pocket and went to the kitchen for the scissors.

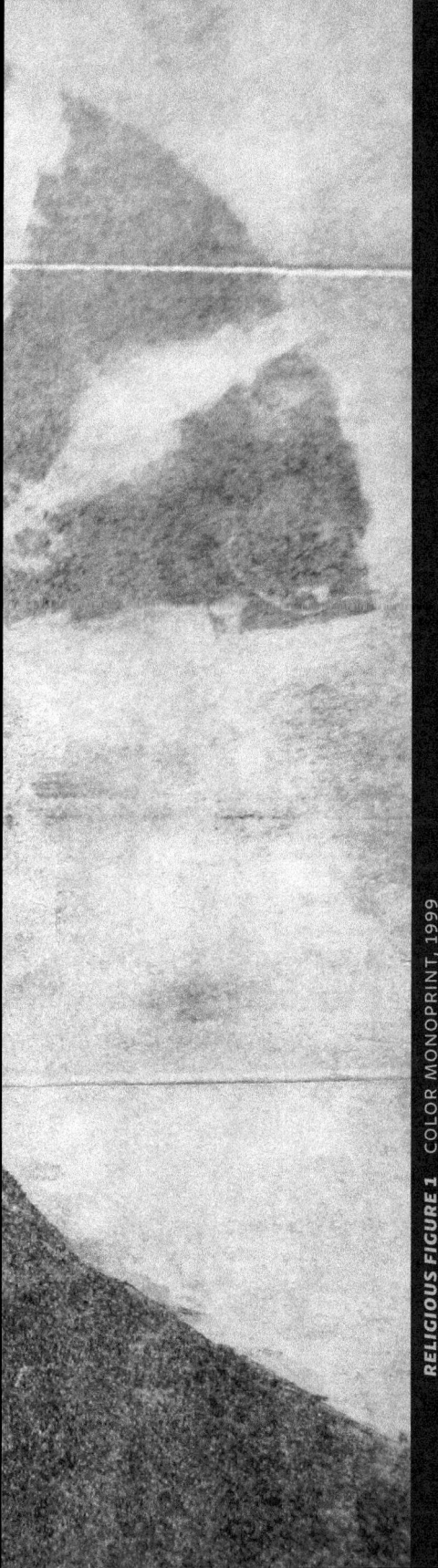

RELIGIOUS FIGURE 1   COLOR MONOPRINT, 1999

Double Exposed

BY ALYSSA WILLIAMS

DIGITAL, 2017

Nothing But Silence

BY ANNA MARTIN

PHOTOGRAPHY, 11 X 17 INCHES, 2014

Crossing in Fog

BY CHRISTOPHER WOODS

DIGITAL, 9 X 12 INCHES, 2017

Monotype and Monoprint

BY JOHN TIMOTHY ROBINSON

CRYING WOMAN

ACTUAL BLOCK USED FOR WOODCUT MONOPRINTS, 2012

ABOVE: *PIONEER CABIN; MOUNT CARMEL RIDGE*, B/W PHOTO, 1999
BELOW: *OLD CAR; MOUNT CARMEL RIDGE*, B/W PHOTO, 1999

WAR FACE, SEPIA MONOTYPE, 1999

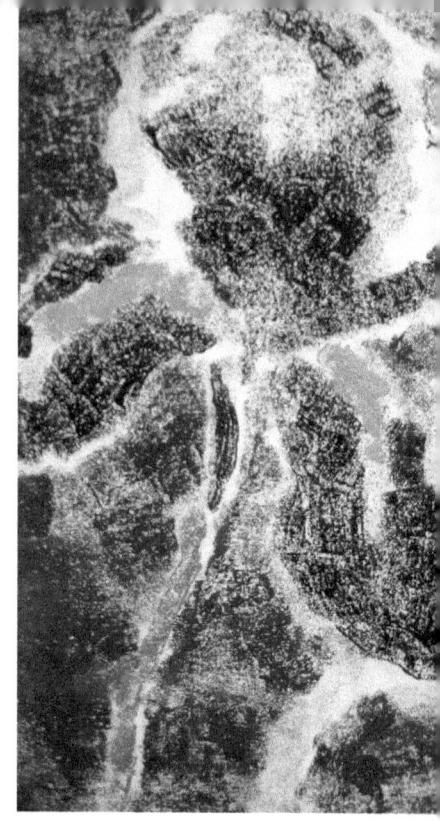

ABOVE LEFT: *THE COOK*, OIL COLOR MONOPRINT, 2011

ABOVE RIGHT: *IRIS; AFTER AYERS; MAGENTA AND YELLOW 1*, 2011

BELOW: *GOLDEN BRIDGE 1*, COLOR BLOCK PRINT MONOPRINT, 2011

ORCHARD KEEPER, COLOR MONOPRINT, 1999

ABOVE: *RELIGIOUS FIGURE 1*, COLOR MONOPRINT, 1999

OPPOSITE: *CANDLE*, MONOTYPE, 1999

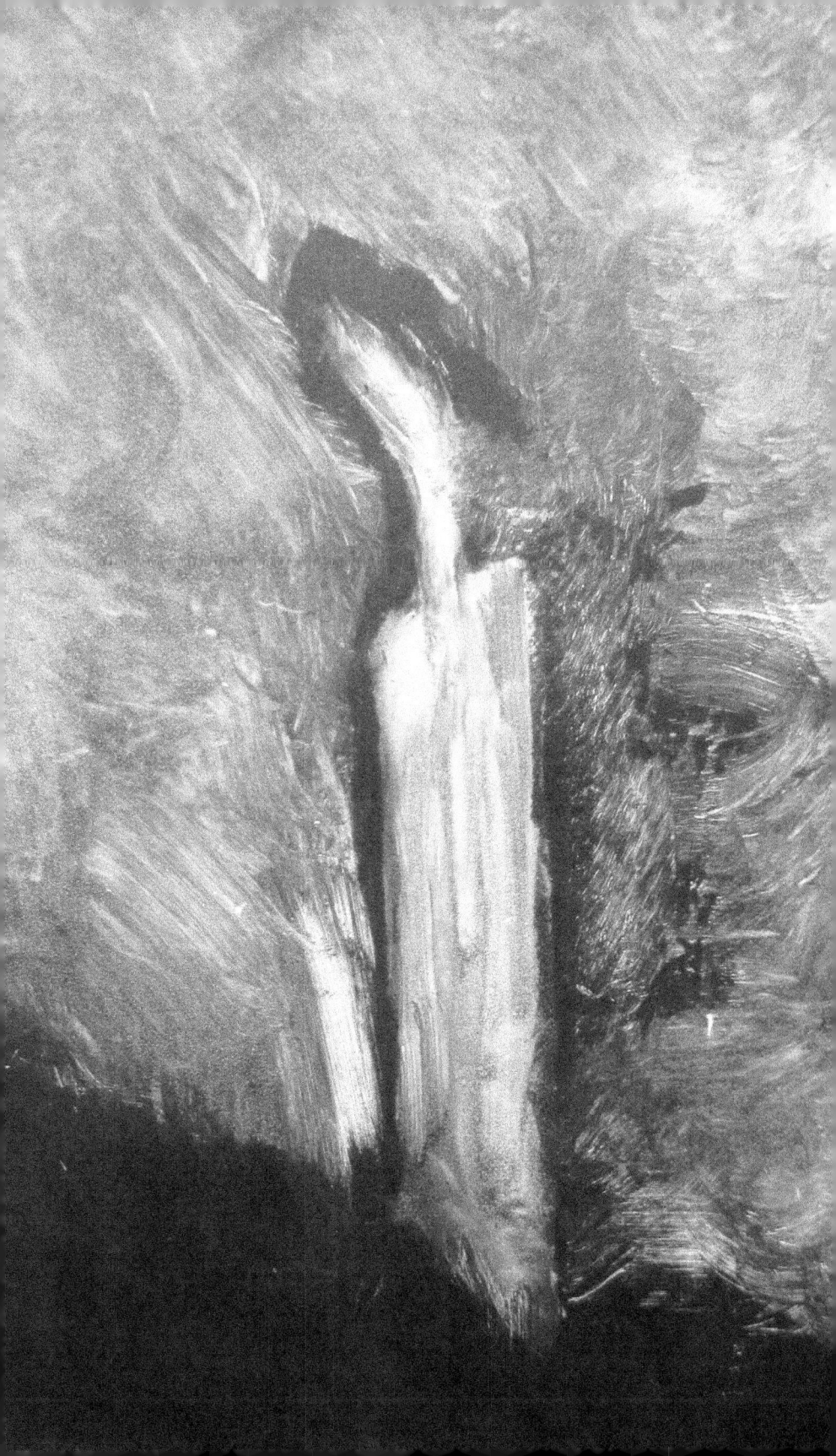

Tomato Menace & Floral Rabbit

BY JURY S. JUDGE

MIXED MEDIA, 16 IN X 20 IN, 2015

Morbidly Bitten

BY JURY S. JUDGE

MIXED MEDIA, 16 IN X 20 IN, 2015

Second Thoughts

BY HOLLY DAY

NEEDLEPOINT, LINEN CANVAS AND COTTON THREAD,
7 X 7 1/2 INCHES

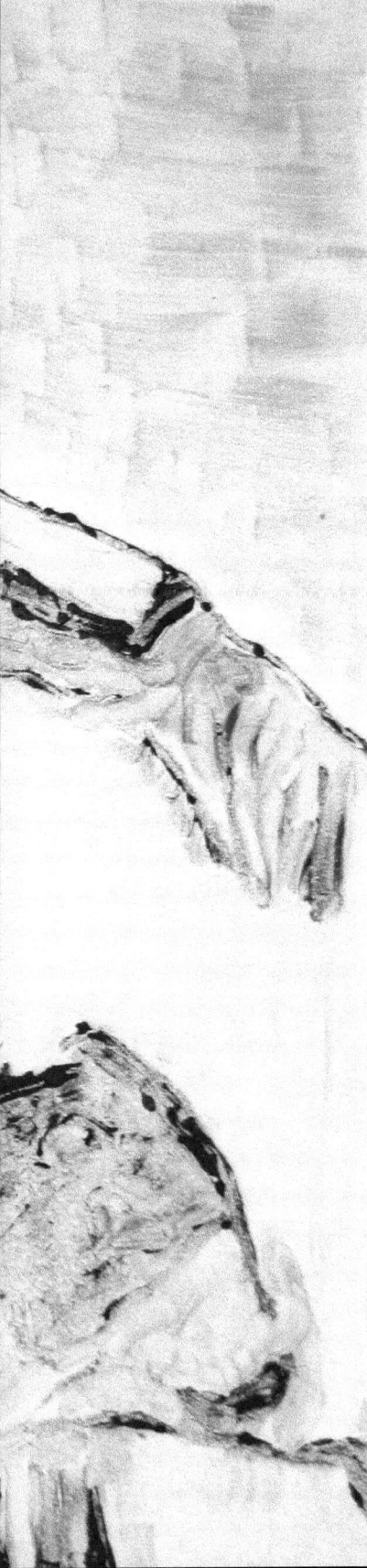

graphic shorts

Positive Resistance

BY JASPER SCHELLEKENS-CARRÉ

INK AND DIGITAL, 2016

Winter Womb

BY JASON HART

DIGITAL, 2017

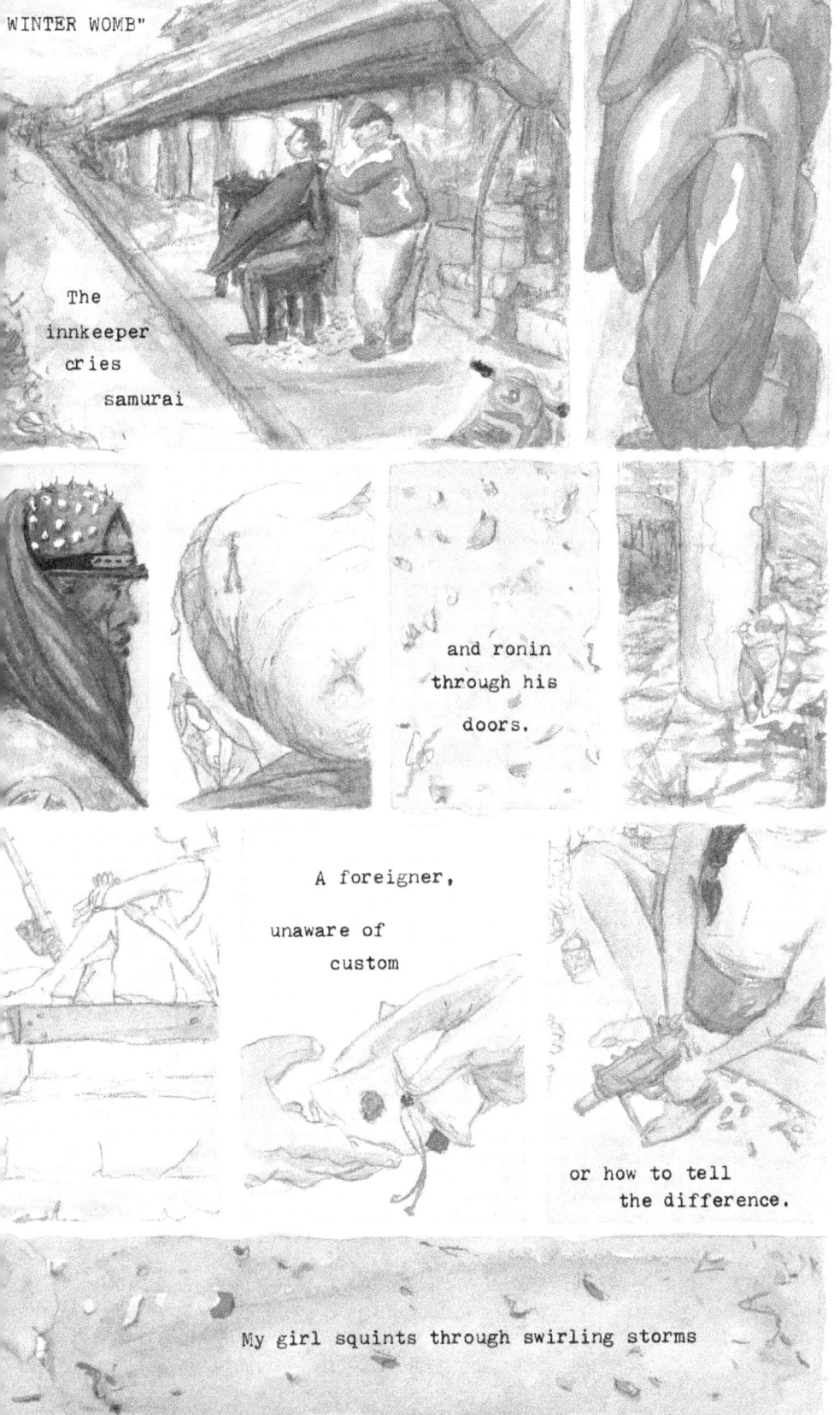

WINTER WOMB"

The
innkeeper
cries
samurai

and ronin
through his
doors.

A foreigner,

unaware of
custom

or how to tell
the difference.

My girl squints through swirling storms

of loss,
in search of home.

Calling, in no distinguishable language,

unsteady in her family tongue.

As I in the dark lie awake and wonder,

Was it good for he

Or overshadowed by the exhaustion,

the clips and shifts and pains

of a fi
trimes

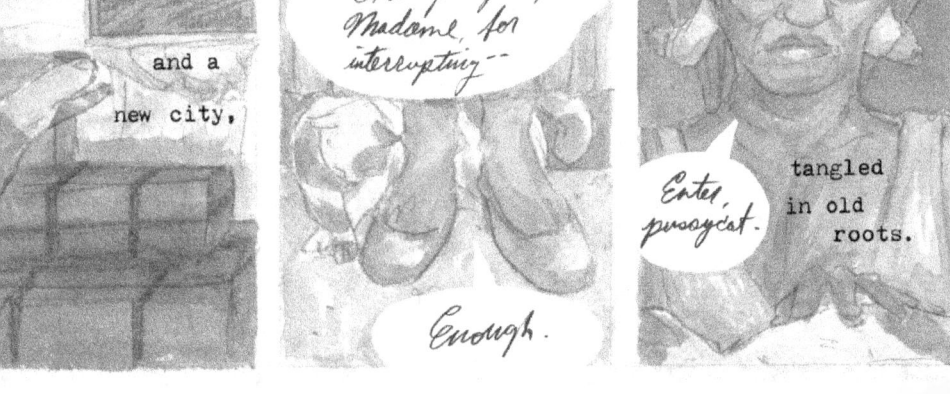

ORCHARD KEEPER COLOR MONOPRINT, 1999

Trust Issues

BY TERESA MIRLL

Lights up on a table in a restaurant. WAYNE *and* JEREMY
sit together. JEREMY *is eating a cheeseburger.*

WAYNE   Then she sends me this text, right? And
she's going on and on about how I have
trust issues. So I start thinking about that,
and after a while, I decide she's full of it.

JEREMY   Well, what happened with Lia? I haven't
seen her since you guys broke up.

WAYNE   I'm not talking about her.

JEREMY   You were just talking about what she said.

WAYNE   No, I don't care about her. I only meant
in general. It's stupid to say I have
trust issues because our entire lives are
founded on trusting other people.

JEREMY   What do you mean?

WAYNE   It's true of everything. I mean anything.
Like, have you ever been on a plane?

JEREMY   Yeah. I went to Colorado once. Got arrested.

WAYNE   What'd you do in Colorado to get arrested?

JEREMY   The guy checking the luggage told me I
had to throw away my on-the-go Nutella
package. That was my only breakfast. So I
punched the guy. Got tackled to the ground.

WAYNE   Well, what I was saying about trust issues
         is that, when you get on a plane, you have
         to trust the pilot to get you where you're
         going, not to decide once he's in the air
         to start doing barrelrolls. And if you go
         to the movies, you trust the guy in the
         projection booth to run the movie, not
         to fall asleep with his cigarette in his
         mouth and set the building on fire.

JEREMY   Oh, okay. Like when you offered to buy lunch,
         I trusted you to drive us to Burger Shack, not
         to slam into a garbage truck or something.

WAYNE   Exactly! And then I bought you lunch like
         I promised. Because you can trust me.

JEREMY   And you can trust me.

WAYNE   Right. The same way I trusted you to
         be on the curb when I drove up.

JEREMY   And how I trusted you not to
         leave me standing in the rain.

WAYNE   Like you trusted my driving in the rain.

JEREMY   And we trusted every other car not to slam
         into us and drive us up onto a mailbox.

WAYNE   See what I mean? It's great, isn't it? It's even
         happening right now. You trust every person
         that went into making that cheeseburger.

JEREMY   Yeah, that's true. I trusted the guy at
         the counter to take my order right.

WAYNE   You trusted the guy at the grill
         to cook it all the way.

JEREMY	I trusted the guy at the counter to bring it to me without dropping it.
WAYNE	Right.
JEREMY	Yeah. That's pretty cool, man.

> JEREMY *takes a bite of his burger.*

WAYNE	But it's so much more than that! I mean, think about your burger alone. You didn't just trust the people who cooked it and brought it to you. You trusted the people in the back to keep the meat cold before they cooked it. You trusted the rancher to raise his cattle right and not give them mad cow disease. You trusted the health department to make sure the bread factory wasn't crawling with rats.

> JEREMY *stops eating.*

WAYNE	You trusted the cheesemaker to let his cheese grow only the right bacteria. You trusted the farmer to spray his lettuce with pesticide to keep bugs off it. You trusted the people back there in the kitchen to wear their gloves while they worked, not to scratch their faces or their heads or shake hands with some dude that just got done—
JEREMY	Come on, man!

> JEREMY *drops the burger and pushes it away.* LIA *the waitress enters behind* JEREMY, *carrying a sundae.*

She approaches JEREMY *and*
WAYNE. WAYNE *looks at* LIA.

WAYNE You trust the waitress not to spit in your
sundae. You trust the waitress not to slam
you in the head with a brick and steal
your wallet. You trust her to spend an
evening partying with her friends and not
make out with random guys in the club.

JEREMY *turns as* LIA
stops beside the table.

JEREMY Oh—

WAYNE You trust the waitress not to cheat
on you the minute you trust her
enough to have your back turned.

LIA *looks at* WAYNE.

LIA Watcha talking about?

WAYNE Trust issues.

LIA Oh, okay. Trusting people. Like how you
trust the customer to tip you. You trust the
customer to take the sundae, not dump it on
your head. You trust the customer to realize
that Cindy Villanueva is a liar who cheated
on him and who still texts him all the time
even though they broke up a year ago. You
trust the customer not to come to your
job when he knows you work just to talk
trash about you while you're on the clock.

LIA *turns to* JEREMY.

JEREMY	Lia, I swear, I had no idea you worked here.

LIA	Is this your sundae?

JEREMY	Yes.

LIA	Good, then I don't have to spit in it.

> LIA *sets the sundae down on the table.*

WAYNE	You trust Cindy's boyfriend, Todd, to tell you the truth about what they both saw in the club.

LIA	You trust your boyfriend to ask you about a rumor, not an ex-girlfriend and some guy your boyfriend's never met.

WAYNE	You trust a stranger who doesn't have a reason to lie over some waitress who would want to hide the lie.

LIA	You trust your boyfriend to realize that Todd would literally do anything if Cindy asked him to.

WAYNE	You trust any guy on the planet not to help his girlfriend get back together with her ex.

LIA	You trust your boyfriend to realize Todd would grovel on the ground in a banana suit if it meant getting some from Cindy! But speaking of the kiss in the club—

> LIA *leans down and kisses* JEREMY *on the cheek.*

LIA	You trust your boyfriend to know that doesn't count as making out with someone. You trust him to look at Amanda's party photos, which show you kissing Mark on the cheek. You trust your boyfriend to remember that Mark has known he was gay since he was ten and that Mark once got drunk and hit on your boyfriend.
WAYNE	You trust your boyfriend not to have Amanda's number because he wouldn't cheat on you!
LIA	You trust your boyfriend to trust you!

LIA *looks at* JEREMY.

LIA	You trust Jeremy to get Wayne out of here, right now.

LIA *exits.*

JEREMY	Dude.
WAYNE	Oh, sure, just sit there in silence. Again.
JEREMY	What do you want me to say?
WAYNE	Some support would be nice. Maybe a little sympathy. Maybe an "Oh, man, that sucks, bro" or something.
JEREMY	I don't know what happened at the club! I wasn't there!
WAYNE	You didn't have to be there!
JEREMY	Come on, man.

WAYNE	Or you could believe me when I tell you what happened.
JEREMY	Well, what if Lia's right? What if that Cindy chick is trying to get you back? Or maybe she's still mad about your break-up last year, so she went out of her way to make you and Lia break up. How do I know?
WAYNE	You trust your best friend to have your back.
JEREMY	You trust your best friend to tell you if the place where he's dragging you to lunch is where his ex-girlfriend works.
WAYNE	You trust him to understand what you're going through.
JEREMY	You trust him to think about what he just put you through.
WAYNE	You trust your best friend to help you get past this.
JEREMY	You trust him not to start a fight in the middle of Burger Shack that ambushes you and his ex-girlfriend.
WAYNE	You trust your best friend to be on your side.
JEREMY	You trust your best friend not to be a jerk.
WAYNE	You trust him not to ditch you at Burger Shack and make you walk home three blocks in the rain!

WAYNE *stands and walks away.*

JEREMY   You trust Wayne not to be a jerk, but he is!

                    WAYNE *exits.*

WAYNE   *(Calling from offstage)* You trust your
              best friend to care about you!

JEREMY   You trust him to care about you
              walking two miles in the rain!

WAYNE   *(Calling from offstage)* You trust
              him to care about caring!

                    A doorbell tinkles. Beat.
                    JEREMY *stands and*
                    walks toward the door.

JEREMY   You trust the rain to let up soon.

                    JEREMY *returns to the table.*
                    He looks down at his sundae.

JEREMY   It melted.

                    LIA *enters, carrying a*
                    sundae on a tray. She
                    approaches JEREMY.

LIA   Here. Made you a new one.

JEREMY   Thanks.

LIA   Yeah, I figured that one would be ruined
          by the time you actually got to eat it.

                    JEREMY *pushes away*
                    the first sundae. LIA sets
                    down the new one.

LIA	And also, I thought that one was Wayne's, so I spit in it.
JEREMY	Did you know the burger was mine?
LIA	No.

JEREMY retches.

LIA	No, I mean I wasn't here. When I got back from my last break, Fred asked me to make a sundae for the guy at table two. I thought he pointed at Wayne.
JEREMY	Is Fred a trustworthy guy?
LIA	He's a germ freak. And he's obsessive about checking temps and keeping everything clean. He's gunning for kitchen manager.
JEREMY	That's a relief. Still not sure about the farmer, though.
LIA	What?
JEREMY	Nothing.

JEREMY looks around at the empty dining room.

JEREMY	So, you wanna sit for a while?

LIA looks behind her and then sits.

LIA	Yeah, Fred and Keith have the kitchen. So for real, what are you talking about, "you're not sure about the farmer?"

JEREMY	That whole trust thing Wayne was saying. You trust the farmer to raise the cows right.
LIA	He's right, I suppose. Even though he's just saying "everybody trusts somebody" to pretend that he's not a total scumbag.
JEREMY	Well, yeah, before he start—I mean, at first I thought it was a great idea. It was really cool to think about. I trust the person who made my ice-cream. Who made this table. And this chair. The building hanging over us right now. We're all sitting here trusting the ceiling not to cave in on us right now.

LIA *looks up.*

LIA	Scary.
JEREMY	Well, yeah, that's the problem. You have to trust people. Sometimes they do what you hope they will, and sometimes they screw you over and laugh while they're doing it. They ditch you at Burger Shack and tell you you're a bad person.
LIA	Well, I guess you can't do anything about it when that happens. You can't just stop trusting people because of one emotionally-manipulative jerkweed. If you really did stop trusting everybody, you'd end up living out in the forest in a hole you dug in the ground, scrounging for beetles and snarling at anybody who came near you.
JEREMY	Not the best plan.

| LIA | Besides, there are so many good things that come out of trusting people. What about when you let some lady cut in front of you in line and then she pays your bill for you? Or if you trust a guy not to kill you on the first date, what if you end up falling in love for the next fifty years? You trust people all the time, and maybe that's not a bad thing. Like trusting friends and family to help you when you're stuck. |

LIA stands.

LIA	You trust the waitress to give you a ride home so you don't have to walk in the rain.
JEREMY	Thanks, Lia.
LIA	Not a problem. Back in twenty.

LIA exits. Lights fade.

prose

CRYING WOMAN ACTUAL BLOCK USED FOR WOODCUT MONOPRINTS, 2012

Almost

BY KELLY GROGAN

MILES PICKED UP THE PHONE AFTER SEVERAL rings, assuming his manager was calling to ask him about the past-due analytics, but it was Camilla calling. It was her birthday, and she wanted to see him. Miles agreed to meet at her apartment in Beacon Hill at eight o'clock, and then called Hannah and told her he needed to work late, not to wait up for him. "They're saying the office is going to be closed tomorrow," he said, "because of the snow." The lie slipped out easily but not without a pang of guilt. For a moment he imagined his wife, standing alone at the window in their unlit house watching the snow fall. A moment only, and then it passed.

Even though it was true that he had some work to finish up, Miles couldn't concentrate. He scrolled through his emails without reading anything and at six-thirty he gave in and left the office, deciding to walk to Camilla's instead of taking the train. He thought it would take longer that way, but even with the slow movement of the crowds he ended up wandering through the Boston Commons by Camilla's apartment with nearly an hour to pass. He watched a group of ice skaters spin and glide around the rink in the middle of the park. Snowflakes stung his face each time the wind lifted.

He used to ice skate in the winter. He'd skated backwards, holding Hannah's hands in his own while the two of them wobbled unsteadily along the perimeter of the rink. Then, with their son—as a child Lucas stood tightly between them, one hand in each of theirs; when he grew up, he flew past them, never looking backwards, always racing faster, faster. Lucas had skated like the boy Miles watched now, circling the rink alone in a blue coat. In the blur of his movement the boy looked just like Lucas would have—he was the right age, the right height, his hair was a mess of curls. Except Lucas was gone. Even though it'd been two years, Miles still had to remind himself of that.

Miles shivered and glanced at his watch, turning away from the ice skaters and walking along the edge of the crowd to the north side of the park. Across the street, a small market glowed through the dark and he went inside, if only to thaw himself out for a few minutes. It struck him as he entered and scanned the store that should get a gift for Camilla's birthday. Miles drifted through the wine aisle, scanning the rows of bottles lining the shelves. Camilla had ordered red wine when they met at the restaurant last week, but what kind? Merlot? He couldn't remember. Reading the labels, Miles felt suddenly too warm, weighted down in his damp clothing.

As he turned to leave, a splash of color caught his eye, a bucket of flowers, their bright blossoms contrasting with the darkness beyond the window. He sifted through the bouquets and picked a slender bundle of orange, yellow, and red flowers. The clerk tugged a plastic bag over the buds, a barrier against the snow. Miles carried the bouquet through the Commons and up the steep hill to Camilla's apartment, avoiding the patches of black ice that slicked across the brick sidewalks.

After pressing the buzzer to Camilla's apartment, he waited outside, brushing the snow from his coat and stamping ice from his shoes. The plastic bag covering the flowers was dimpled with melting snowflakes and he tugged it off and rolled it into a ball, stuffing it into his coat pocket. A few snowflakes drifted onto the flowers and turned into dew. He cradled the flowers against his chest, hugging them as though he could keep them warm. Miles pressed the buzzer again, longer this time, and cleared his throat. "Camilla?" he called into the intercom. "It's me, Miles. Are you there?" After another moment, the door buzzed and he walked up the narrow stairway to her apartment.

Camilla barely noticed when the bell rang, so immersed was she in the swirls of her painting. She dabbed the tip of her brush against the canvas in small, gentle strokes, her face pressed close to the details. Her palette was thick with globs of cadmium, crimson, and vermillion, all brushed through with zinc. The bell rang again and Miles's voice called out through the intercom, scratchy and distant. Camilla sighed and sat back, setting her paintbrush on the table. Why had she invited him in the first place? She should have known she'd get caught up in painting, that she wouldn't want to be disturbed. But it was her birthday. It wasn't right to spend it alone. Allowing herself one last glance at her work, Camilla walked to the entry and let Miles up.

When she opened the door to greet him, Miles held out a wilted bouquet of daisies, their petals drooping. His face was flushed pink from the wind and Camilla thought of her painting, the warmth of the sunset reflected in the water, the wisps of clouds stretching across the sky to the edge of the canvas. She almost said to him, then, that she'd made a mistake calling. She almost told him to go home. She could have used the excuse of the storm, told him she wouldn't want him to get stuck there.

But it was too late. Miles walked through the doorway and held out the bouquet. "Happy Birthday," he said, and she instinctively took the flowers and raised them to her face. They smelled sour, tinged with the scent of the cellophane. The daisies were red and orange—not the subtle, shifting hues of her paints, but saturated and artificial, like they'd had food coloring in their water. She glanced up at Miles, and she kissed him lightly on the cheek. "Thanks," she said. "Come in, come in."

While Miles peeled off his coat and scarf, Camilla carried the flowers to her kitchen. She filled a slender vase with warm water and stuffed the daisies inside. When she bought flowers for herself, she always chose bouquets that were light-colored and delicate—carnations or lilies, hydrangeas, peonies. Occasionally, in spring, after so many months of winter, she would bring home bright, creamy daffodils, their faces round and yellow like the sun. But how could she expect Miles to know what flowers she liked? She should be grateful for the daisies, and grateful to him for coming over.

Miles coughed from the living room, and Camilla called out to him. "Can I get you a glass of wine? I have a Malbec that's nice."

"Yes," he said, his voice echoing from the living room. "Malbec. Of course."

She pulled two long-stemmed glasses from the cabinet and filled them, splashing a bit extra in both. She paused beside the vase of flowers on her way out of the kitchen, then scooped it up in the crook of her elbow, the petals brushing against her neck while she walked to the living room.

Miles was standing beside the bay windows, silhouetted in falling snow, his head bent while he watched the street below. The pose was familiar to her, somehow. He did not move when she entered but stood silently with his hands in his pockets until Camilla set the vase on the table with a thump and held out his wineglass. Miles turned to face her and his eyes crinkled into a smile so that he seemed to light up from within at the sight of her, and she found herself smiling back.

Free from his winter layers, Miles felt lighter as he walked into Camilla's living room. In the warmth of her apartment a heaviness settled upon him, all the restlessness and anticipation from the day giving way to a comfortable exhaustion. He walked to the window and traced his fingertips over the veins of frost that formed along the glass. Outside, snow piled up against the buildings and cars in windblown drifts.

An older man shoveled a slim path from the stairs of his building to the sidewalk, and Miles thought that he had to hurry home early enough to spread some salt on his own steps before the snow froze overnight. At the thought of home, another pain of guilt tore through him, just for a second. A vision of his wife lying in their bed at this very moment, reading or watching the weather report with her steaming cup of tea. The framed photo of their son staring out at her with that small, unknowable smile. Before Lucas had died, Hannah would shovel the steps with Miles, pausing to throw snowballs and laughing when he fell into the soft snowbanks. Now he had to do it by himself. He had to shovel, or it would never get done.

Camilla startled him as she set the vase of flowers on the table, and Miles stepped away from the window and faced her with a grin so that she would not ask if anything was wrong. She held out a glass of red wine, and they sat on the couch, her legs curled into his lap. Miles sipped his wine and watched Camilla over the top of the glass. She had been painting, dressed in too-big jeans and a stained Red Sox t-shirt. Her fingers were smudged pink and yellow, and Miles reached across the couch and wiped an orange dot from her cheek, a barely visible freckle in the warm glow of her living room.

"What were you painting?" he asked. Camilla took a long sip of her wine, her gaze flickering to the side of him.

"Nothing," she said, shaking her head and waving her

hand dismissively. "A neighbor commissioned me to do a piece for her husband's birthday next month."

Miles took Camilla's hand in his own, stroking his thumb over the lines of her palm. "What is it a painting of?" he asked, pressing for more. She was distant, she kept glancing at him and then away again.

"It's just a sunset," she said, and paused. "It's cliché, I know. But it's from a photo they took on their honeymoon."

Miles traced a pattern of freckles over her forearm, meeting her eyes. "Can I see it?" he asked, then, "I'd like to."

For a moment, Camilla didn't answer. She looked at the flowers and frowned, barely, almost imperceptibly. Then she smiled at him and wrapped her fingers around his own.

"Ok," she said, standing up and pulling him to his feet. "I can show you. But first, more wine."

As she moved to the kitchen, Miles took her hand and leaned in to kiss her. She pulled back and looked at him and he wondered if he'd done something wrong, if he'd trespassed somehow. But then she brushed her lips against his and took his wineglass, her movements lithe and graceful, and he forgot her hesitation.

As she led Miles through the hallway to her studio, Camilla wondered if he would be able to tell she was lying. She told herself he wouldn't. She reminded herself they'd only met a month ago, only gotten together a handful of times – he didn't know her well enough to catch her in a lie.

Reminding herself again that she had been the one to invite him over, Camilla pushed open the door and walked into the studio. Miles followed, his footsteps heavy on the hardwood floor, and she watched his gaze travel around the room, pretending that she, too, was seeing it for the first time. Empty frames were stacked up along the walls, loose canvas in rolls on the counter, splotches of color on the cement floor, mason jars brimming with liquid along the shelves. It wasn't tidy, but it was organized—Camilla knew where to look when she needed something. She followed Miles's gaze to the center of the room, where the new painting rested on the easel, glistening with thick, oily color.

Miles walked to the painting with his hands behind his back, as though in an art gallery or museum, and his posture struck her again as familiar, and she remembered. It'd been how he stood the night they met—they'd been standing beside each other studying a Degas statue, *The Little Dancer Fourteen Years Old,* at the Museum of Fine Arts. She'd caught his eye through the edge of the dancer's rippling skirt, and that night, over drinks, they talked about the tilt of the dancer's chin, the emboldened, unflinching direction of her gaze. With the lights of Fenway winking around them, the muffled roar of the crowd in the distance, he'd kissed her, suddenly, on the sidewalk. She hadn't stopped him.

When Miles reached Camilla's easel he paused, leaning in to look at the half-finished sunset, his eyes roaming over the canvas. She moved beside him, certain now that he could see the truth—it was not a honeymoon photograph, there was no neighbor, no commission. The sunset was a fragmented moment from her own memory, far away enough to be a dream; and still, even now, a dream that threatened to pull her under if she looked too closely.

Camilla turned her gaze to the window, unable to look at the painting anymore at all. It wasn't right, she could see that now. The oranges were too vivid, the yellows too dark. She'd spent hours hunched over the canvas trying to get the details right and missed the bigger picture—the slant of light curving across the water, the changing hue of the waves. All she'd wanted was to capture the sparkling ocean and the feeling of sand between her toes, to be immersed in the memory of Rachel's flushed smile, her warm hand in Camilla's while they ran into the waves, splashing and laughing in the setting sun. She could have lived in that moment for the rest of her life, suspended, watching it over and over and over. Camilla waited beside the window, and she looked out across the road, snowflakes falling across the streetlights below like so many stars.

Camilla's studio wasn't what Miles had pictured, but then, once he stepped through the doorway he wasn't sure what he'd imagined it would look like. The room itself was bare—white walls and a strong, unforgiving light. Most of the paintings leaning up against the walls were half-finished, some of them marred with a broad, frustrated brushstroke, a colorful erasure. It seemed Camilla often changed her mind mid-painting, or decided to try something different each day. The painting she'd been working on, the sunset for her neighbor, caught his eye from across the room and he walked over to the easel.

This painting was exquisite. It, too, was not yet finished, but somehow Camilla had managed to capture the presence of light. Golden streaks were brushed through the clouds and the swirling water. Looking at the painting felt like falling into a dream, a place a world apart from the gusting wind outside and the icicles that hung from the windows. Even as he turned away from it, the painting lingered in his mind like it'd been imprinted there, a memory of a place he'd almost been to, a place that did not quite exist. He could picture, there, the sound of his son laughing; and Hannah, no longer the ghost of the woman he'd married, taking his hand in her own. The distant vision of a life that receded inevitably into the past. A world erased and redrawn. He wondered what Camilla saw, what memories lay hidden for her that so illuminated her work.

Miles glanced up at her. She stood beside the window with her back to him. He absentmindedly picked up a paintbrush from the table, rolling it between his fingers. Then, almost without realizing he was doing it, he slid the paintbrush deep into his pocket.

When Camilla glanced at him, Miles straightened and smiled at her, hoping she hadn't noticed. "It's stunning," Miles said, gesturing toward the painting. "Your neighbor will be really happy."

He walked to her and wrapped an arm around her back, pulling her close and breathing in the perfume of her, the scent of wine and linseed oil and beeswax. She wove her fingers through his own, her touch warm, and kissed him.

"Should we go to the bedroom?" she asked, and he nodded into her neck.

As they walked back through the studio doorway, Miles noticed something beneath a shelf in the corner, something that'd fallen or been swept into the shadows. He bent down and picked it up, shaking the dust off. It was a mask with ebony satin, striped feathers, and elaborate patterns of beads woven around the edges. A string of dark pearls was wrapped loosely around the thin handle—real pearls, imperfect and round.

Miles held up the mask as he followed Camilla to the bedroom and when she saw it her lips parted for a second, her eyes glinting with something he didn't recognize. So quickly that he wasn't sure he really saw it, just a flash, then Camilla smiled as she took the mask from him.

"Oh, I forgot about this," she said, running her fingers over the soft edges of the feathers, the uneven pearls. "Where did you find it?" She turned to the mirror without waiting for an answer and held the mask up over her face, studying her reflection. That delicate movement, her eyes lifting, the angle of her chin—it was as though the mask were made for Camilla.

He kissed her and the feathers brushed against him, but when he reached up to tug the mask away she stopped him. Camilla pulled back and looked at him through the mask, not blinking—what she thought then, what she saw, Miles didn't know. She looked at once bemused and sad. He brushed his hand against her cheek, letting his fingers graze her lips, then he kissed her again. Camilla's voice was soft in his ear, her hair tangled into his fingers.

Camilla kept her eyes closed while they lay together, entwined in the sheets. She felt as though she'd stood at the edge of some precipice and then plunged in, to a space cold and bottomless. She sank into the feeling, deeper and deeper, like she was falling into a dream. Perhaps this was the reason she'd called Miles earlier, the reason she'd slept with him that first night in Fenway—the feeling of falling while they stood on either side of the dancer statue, inching toward each other step by step. It was the opposite of the gravity that had tugged at the soles of her feet the summer she met Rachel: that long, warm, Californian summer together, lying head to head in the sand while sunlight spilled around them. With the sapphire ocean stretched out before them it'd been easy to let herself fall in love, easy to miss the signs—the marks on Rachel's arms, the tiny puncture wounds where needles left bruises behind, the way she'd disappear for days at a time. All Camilla noticed were the blue skies, the way their bodies tangled together in front of the fan when the Santa Ana winds blew at night, the feeling of the sun in her skin. She thought about how she and Miles had met each other in the middle of a vast emptiness, their hands outstretched, trying just to touch.

Miles stirred beneath her arm, sitting up.

"What are you thinking about?" he asked.

"Nothing," she said, and ran her hand across his knee. Nothing—just as Rachel had said, all those years ago, the last time she saw her. *Nothing, dear Camill-ia*—that's what Rachel called her, Camellia, like the flower, the extra syllable sending a shiver through her whenever she heard it.

Camilla rolled toward the edge of the bed, searching for her clothes. "What are *you* thinking about?" she asked.

"Nothing," he said, taking her hand. Then, "I need some water."

She climbed off the bed and pulled on her clothes, the soft t-shirt hugging her bare skin. Rachel's mask lay crumpled on the floor at the foot of the bed, and Camilla picked it up, smoothing the feathers out. It had been so strange, to wear it—for a moment, she had not recognized herself at all.

Camilla set the mask on her bureau and walked back to Miles, handing him his shirt. She had already begun thinking again about the painting again, disappointed at the way the colors looked faded and the towering clouds had turned out flat and lifeless. No matter how delicate her brushstrokes and how accurate her blending of color, the painting would never compare to the memory.

Camilla almost turned to Miles to ask him to stay, to pretend the snow was too deep to walk through, pretend the trains were shut down already, pretend they had no choice but to spend the night together. She didn't want to be alone. Not tonight. But the empty-eyed mask stared at her from her dresser and she could not bring herself to ask.

For a moment, while he stood in the entry and wrapped himself back up layer by layer, Miles thought that Camilla might ask him to stay. He wanted her to ask. He thought about sleeping beside her while the snow buried the world outside. His own house had been an empty shell for so many years; the sadness was palpable, he sometimes felt he could not breathe. As he pulled on his coat and his boots, stepping through the melted snow that pooled on the floor, Miles met Camilla's eyes and he pleaded silently for her to ask him to stay. But her smiles were too quick and her silences too long, her eyes staring past him, always past him, like she was somewhere else. He searched her face for some betrayal of feeling, some secret signal, but he couldn't read anything in her eyes. She was as much a stranger to him then as she was the night they'd met.

Outside Camilla's apartment, Miles fumbled through his pockets to find his phone, to see if Hannah had called. He pulled out the crumpled plastic bag that'd covered the flowers, still damp, and tossed it into the snow. There were no missed calls, but he thought he should call her, so he dialed home. The phone rang unanswered, and Miles was struck suddenly with a sharp stab of fear. Perhaps Hannah was not home. Perhaps she'd run away, or gone to a hotel with a bottle of her sleeping pills, or she had followed Lucas, gone into his bedroom where his books were still strewn on the desk, gone into the room where the memory of his body still hung in the closet. He had not known his son was dead, would not have guessed until the moment he saw him there. He called again, more frantically, and then, she answered. Her voice was tired, groggy. Miles had woken her up.

"What's wrong?" Hannah said, and he heard the rustle of the blankets. He breathed a long sigh of relief, his breath hanging like fog in the air before him.

"Nothing, nothing," he said. "I'm sorry I woke you. I'm just calling to say I'm on my way home. I'll be there soon."

"Ok," Hannah said. There was a silence, a vague static like snowflakes against the window.

"I love you," Miles said.

"You too." A click.

Miles rounded the sidewalk and walked to the train station, sniffling in the cold wind, his hands in his pockets. At the edge of his fingertips, he could feel the paintbrush he'd taken from Camilla's studio. By now, Camilla had probably forgotten Miles completely, gone back to painting as she'd wanted to all along. He thought he should toss the paintbrush aside, let it be buried in the snowfall like the plastic bag. Instead, he put it back in his pocket, rolling it back and forth between his forefinger and thumb.

After she closed the door and Miles's footsteps faded down the stairway, Camilla leaned against the wall, closing her eyes. She listened to the thud of the door closing, and the silence that followed. When she moved again, she walked to the living room and took the flowers from the vase and carried them to the trash, their many-colored petals falling in clumps into the bin. Then she returned to her studio and sat down before the painting, staring at it for a moment before dipping the tip of her paintbrush into a dab of crimson paint and dragging it in a single line across the sky, ruining all her work, all those hours she'd spent hunched over the colors. She walked to the window and looked outside again, feeling for a moment like she was peering out from the inside of a snow globe, the lights of windows twinkling out in the distance. The dark and bare limbs of the trees were heavy with snow and icicles clung to the eaves of the rooftops across the street. When Rachel died, the rain poured for nearly three weeks without stopping, flooding the creeks and the gutters. As though the sky knew what to sculpt out of Camilla's sadness. Tonight, the world was cold and empty, but beautiful still.

Perhaps she should have asked Miles to stay. He'd stood in the doorway wrapped in so many layers, hesitating as he always did before saying goodnight. She could have asked, and he would have said yes.

Camilla returned to her easel, moving the ruined sunset painting to the floor and replacing it with a new canvas, blank, ready for color.

When Miles reached the station, he stood at the top of the escalator, the rumble of the subway moving beneath him, and decided to walk to the next stop. He passed the market where he'd bought the flowers, now closed, its lights turned off. The flowers, their bright petals spreading open in Camilla's living room. The elegant shape of the black feather mask and her eyes looking out from within; the painting of a sunset, a window into another world, to a place both foreign and familiar.

He could have asked to stay. If he'd stayed, Miles would be listening to Camilla murmuring in her sleep, the warmth of her filling his mind, leaving no room for thoughts or memories. He could still go back. Turn around, knock on her door, go into her apartment and refuse to leave. Miles pulled his coat tight around him, hunched against the wind with his fingers wrapped around the paintbrush inside his pocket. When he reached the next station, he walked on, barely pausing beside the entrance before continuing forward. He would get a train eventually. But for now, the streets were empty and the snowflakes clouded the road before him, erasing everything, making the way unclear.

In Winter

BY LESLIE DAVIS

*F*OR REASONS HE COULDN'T EXPLAIN, JEB expected it to be warmer. He'd left his log house, wearing just a lightweight parka and tweed cap. The forsythia was in bud. The dogwood might open any day, and Buddy wandered out ahead, nosing through the beds of newly thawed earth that Clara had sown years ago. Jeb pulled his collar close around his neck and headed down the lane.

A neighbor, Sam Wilkes, waved his cap, hoping to get Jeb's attention. Glad for the familiar face, Jeb called out, "Hullo there." When he'd gotten close enough, they tossed a few words back and forth about what a nippy morning it was. Sam had pulled his cap down over the tips of his ears. He patted the front of his down vest, and asked Jeb if he wasn't a bit chilly.

"A little snap in the air never hurt anyone. Besides, I'm a tough old bird."

The dog wagged over to the man. "Well, hel-lo ole Bud," Sam said, and ruffed the retriever's dull coat. When he stood straight again, he said, "Saw Ellen leaving your place the other week. She waved from the car. Reckon those boys of hers must be a handful. Probably running her ragged now she's on her own?"

The last time his daughter Ellen had been by was just days before. Like always, she'd let herself in, wearing that prying smile of hers that, for Jeb, was always the most memorable detail of her visits.

"That's about right," he said, "them running her. But not so hard as to keep her out of my hair."

"Aw," Sam batted his hand at nothing, "don't know how good you got it. Hell, we'd be lucky to hear from Lindsey once, twice a year."

Jeb shook his head.

"I know what I wanted to ask you." Sam edged the fleece-lined cap off his brow. "You seen that black bear around here lately—the one kept coming around before the snows last year? Had her half-grown cubs in tow."

"Nope. Can't say as I have."

"Will said he spotted her down at the creek a day or two ago. She was alone."

"Well. I always keep my pea-shooter handy," Jeb said. "Just never know."

Sam chuckled. "No need worrying about you, then. What did you say you were? A tough old bird?" He clapped Jeb's shoulder, then glanced at his watch. "Look, gotta run. Playing chauffeur today."

Jeb mulled it over, but couldn't come up with the wife's name. "You give her my best, hear?"

"Will do," said Sam. "Will do."

Jeb lay in bed, dreaming of mallard season. In his dream, he was itching to get out to his blind—the tight row of Fraser firs from which he'd have a clear shot, and take the greenheads by surprise.

They were skirting the clearing, he and Buddy, closing in on the creek—the gurgle now louder than before. But Jeb couldn't shake the sensation that it was they who were being stalked. Even with the Frasers in view, he and Buddy diverted widely from the path, snaking their way evasively through the wood. Only when he'd heard the snap of a twig did Jeb spin 'round. There she was, the black bear. She'd reared on her hindquarters and towered above him.

What woke him then, from his fitful sleep, seemed distant at first, less real to him than his bear. But the whimpering and scratching at the front door got him up, and Jeb felt his way through the darkened rooms. When he parted the curtains, he was dumbfounded. How long had his Buddy been out there in the cold? He fumbled with the knob, and the door swung in, knocking him against the wall as the dog pushed past.

"I don't know what else to do, Dad." Ellen was seated at the kitchen table. She was going through Jeb's pill bottles, refilling the seven-day dose box when she'd introduced the unmentionable: taking a tour of Mountain View Elder Estates in neighboring McDowell County.

Just who did she think she was to suggest he leave his home? The home where he'd lived for some eighty-odd years. There was a day when he'd have sent her to her room.

"The thing is, you're still forgetting to take your pills," she'd gone on. "I just can't get out here as often as I'd like. As often as you *need*."

"Damn it, Ellen! What I don't *need* is you coming around here thinking you're gonna wipe my nose. Got that?"

He watched from the window while she pulled on her galoshes and took up the umbrella she'd left on the stoop to dry. From behind, she looked like Clara, as Jeb remembered her. And in that moment, he regretted what he'd said.

When Ellen had gone, Jeb lifted his jacket off the hook and went out to sit in one of the porch rockers. His shotgun leaned next to the door where he often left it. Buddy had followed him out and lay at his feet.

He'd thought it out so many years ago, back when his old man had lost his marbles. It was why Jeb kept his peashooter loaded—never for bears like he'd told Sam. Hell, it was loaded so he'd have some kind of control—go out on his own terms, maybe with a little dignity intact. The only flaw he could see in the plan was knowing when it was time. He figured he'd need to be well on this side of it to make it work. Still, there'd always be the risk that he'd fool himself into believing it was too soon.

"The key, Buddy boy," he said, glancing at the retriever, "is not to wait too long."

He was barefoot and in his pajamas when he'd gone outside in the first light. Jeb wasn't cold as he stooped beneath the window, holding Buddy back from the set of prints, undisturbed yet in the loam. She'd been there. It *wasn't* just a dream. The imprints of fleshy pads, the deep scores left behind by her impressive claws, were proof.

On two earlier occasions, she'd stared in at him through the kitchen window. Even if he couldn't locate her visits on a calendar, he could recall each with eerie clarity—her black face bathed in the lamplight from his table, her strong, brown muzzle, and the shiny nose that twitched with curiosity as she fogged the panes with measured breath.

On each of the three nights, they'd locked eyes. Hers, intelligent and knowing. That they'd come to an understanding gave Jeb comfort.

As the old man and his dog tramped through the wood, dry leaves rattled above in the all-but-bare willows. Where had summer gone? Fall? He had no recollection of their passing and shivered at the notion that he was out of phase.

Buddy was leading him out to the lake. Jeb had his shotgun over his shoulder. His pintail whistle hung off the lanyard 'round his neck. Mallards circled above the still water.

When he and Buddy had reached the blind, Jeb crouched and waited. And not until the flock was well downwind did he draw his whistle and call them back. The sound of the shotgun discharging scattered the birds beyond the borders of the lake, and in their confused flapping, they seemed trapped under the low dome of gray sky.

Buddy had swam out across the icy cold to retrieve the felled drake. But when he'd ferried it nearly to the bank, he came no further—standing then shin deep on the shoal—deaf to Jeb's commands. Still, Buddy held the limp bird obediently in his soft jaws.

As the old man made his way toward the water's edge, he saw just how thin the dog was. Its yellow fur, dripping wet, molded to protruding ribs. Buddy dropped the drake onto the shale, but when Jeb approached, the dog growled and snapped it up again, trotting to a safe distance as Jeb sank to his knees. When was it he'd fed Buddy last? Jeb clutched at the pang of his own craving. The dog glared at him. Its teeth bore into the grey feathers, splitting them down to the belly.

There was a vague sense of Ellen bringing meals. "Lasagna's in the fridge, okay?" But the emptiness in his gut spoke loudest, and while Jeb gazed at the half-starved dog, he knew he couldn't trust himself—that he wasn't able to protect Buddy anymore.

Before the thought could get away, Jeb raised the shotgun and welded it to his cheek. He swung the barrel upward, spotting something on the ridge that he ignored, and completed his pan of the shagbark hickories on the far side of the basin. Buddy was still at work on the mallard when Jeb aligned the aperture. The dog tensed at the flip of the safety, but with one clean shot he was down.

The further Jeb distanced himself from the lake, the further the morning's revelations receded. And by the time he was winding his way up the rocky slope, all memory of the day's events had fallen away. Jeb roamed the edge of the creek with the single-mindedness of an animal, days without a kill. Surely Clara would have eggs and toast waiting. The thought of this cheered the old man, and he went lightly on his way.

The Rodeo Monkey

BY SHAWN CAMPBELL

THE MONKEY WAS DRESSED LIKE A COWBOY. Chaps, vest, and a little hat tied onto his head with a piece of string. He rode a Border Collie with a specially fitted saddle. The dog was young, exuberant, and specifically trained not to mind the extra load on its back. The clowns sent the monkey and his dog into the arena between events. The duo had a number of tricks. The dog would herd a group of goats back into a pin or jump over a series of straw bales. The monkey would hang grimly on to the dog's back, occasionally raking his miniature spurs down the dog's back to get it to go faster. Sometimes the monkey would pull out a little pop gun, which he would shoot into the air or at targets held by the clowns, who would fall in mock agony with every hit.

Dusty loved the monkey. Every time the monkey would charge out on his canine steed Dusty would give out a little eight-year-old squeal of delight and tug frantically at his mother's arm, pointing as he tried to get her attention.

"Mom. Mom. Look at the monkey."

Each time, Linda would smile and hold her son close, pressing her cheek to his for a moment, and watch the running dog with the monkey on his back. Dusty would clap and cheer, and the world would fill with so much happiness that, for a moment, Linda would feel herself be carried away to the unbridled enthusiasm of her own childhood. But such times were fleeting. The monkey would ride back out of the arena, and the next event would begin. Dusty would quiet down and watch, bored by the non-monkey related competitions.

Linda didn't watch the rodeo. She stared down at the beer garden and tried to discern the shape of her husband amongst the convulsing sea of western shirts and cowboy hats. The sweaty heat of the afternoon had given way to the chill of evening. Linda had hoped that the drop in temperature would be enough to force her husband back to the grandstands, at least to get his coat, but there was no such luck. Dave was a man impervious to climate, especially while imbibing. Dave had left them and escaped into his sanctuary as soon as they had arrived in the early afternoon. He preferred the company of drunks and fools to that of his own son and wife.

Linda thought she saw him for a second, but the man was too thin, his shirt the only thing he had in common with Dave. She looked at her son, who was intently watching the last round of calf roping, breaking only for an occasional yawn or to pop a candy in his mouth. She could see Dave in her head, laughing and buying drinks for anyone who would claim to be his friend. Spending money they couldn't afford to spend. Linda had once been part of that world and had reveled in it. Now it seemed like those memories belonged to a different woman.

Linda wanted to go home. She had wanted to go home hours ago, but Dave was not so easily roused from his enjoyment. During the second round of barrel racing, she had gone down to the beer garden fence and tried to spy her husband through the drunken mass. She would have gone in to find him herself, but the man at the gate wouldn't let her take Dusty in. She didn't like the idea of leaving Dusty outside by himself. It would take a while to extract Dave when she found him. Instead, she had bought Dusty a hot dog and taken him back to their seats.

The last round of calf roping would soon be over. It would be followed by the final round of bull riding. Then the rodeo would be over. Linda both looked forward to and dreaded the rodeo's end. Dave would come and find them at least half an hour after the end of the last event, and only then because the beer garden would be closed. He'd come up the grandstand steps, cheerful and laughing, at least until Linda would tell him it was time to go home instead of migrating to the nearest bar. His wishes denied, Dave would either respond by becoming angry and verbose, or sullen and pouty. Either way, there would be a string of backhanded insults coming her way. Worse would be when they got home and she put Dusty to bed. Then would come the groping, the pleading for his marital rights, until she either gave in or he passed out. At times, it seemed easier to just leave him behind. Go home without him. She had done it several times before, but all it had accomplished was a weekend-sized dent in their finances instead of just one day.

"Mom. Mom. It's the monkey again. He's in the parade."

The calf roping had come to an end. The monkey rode out leisurely on his dog. Sitting high in the saddle and pumping his little fist in the air. Behind him came a parade of clowns on tiny wagons pulled by teams of miniature horses. One large, boxy wagon seemed to get stuck in the middle of the arena, and the clowns all gathered around to feign pushing and pulling in an attempt to free it. Fed up, one clown kicked at the wagon with all his exaggerated might. The moment his oversized boot connected with the garishly painted side, fireworks burst from the top, upward into the air, exploding with thunderous booms and bright flashes of color above the arena. The crowd hooted and hollered, and Dusty covered his ears.

The dog did not like the fireworks. At the first thunderous boom, he ran at full speed toward the arena fence, desperate to escape. The monkey holding on for dear life.

The dog jumped through a space between two boards. The monkey tried to crouch lower in his saddle, but the gap was too narrow. The monkey's head kicked back as it hit the top board, and he fell from his mount at the edge of the arena. Several clowns ran towards the monkey. Dusty stood on top of his seat.

"Mom. Mom. What's wrong with the monkey? Is the monkey going to be all right? Mom. Mom."

Linda grabbed Dusty and held him close, turning his face away from the chaos in the arena below. The clowns clustered around the fallen rider. One took off his colorful vest and put it over the body to hide it from view. Linda felt the wetness of her son's tears on her cheek. Dusty tried to wiggle around so that he could see again. Linda picked Dusty up and started carrying him down the grandstand steps. Out of the arena. Past the beer garden. Out of the rodeo grounds. Out to the field, once grass, now dust, filled with rows of cars, pickups, and horse trailers. Linda carried Dusty all the way to their pickup truck. She unlocked the doors, buckled him in, and got into the driver's seat. She put the key in the ignition.

The engine of the pickup stayed silent. Linda let her hand drop to her lap. She couldn't leave Dave. Leaving him was more trouble than it was worth. Linda realized she had left Dave's coat in the stands. For a moment, she thought about going back to get it but didn't. She sat and stared out at the bright lights of the distant arena where the announcer was declaring it was time to start the final round of bull riding. Compared to the voice over the loud-speakers, Dusty's voice sounded small and quiet.

"Is the monkey dead, Mom?"

A hundred motherly answers went through her head, but not one reached her mouth. "Yeah, Dusty. I'm sorry. The monkey's dead."

Dusty started crying, big tears flowing down his cheeks. Linda leaned over and hugged him tightly to her chest. His little hands squeezed her as hard as they could.

"It's okay, baby. It's going to be okay."

"But the monkey's dead." His little voice was choked with emotion.

Linda didn't know what to say. Her brain felt like it had frozen, but when she opened her mouth, the words flowed out like water: "No honey, don't cry, it's okay. He was a bad monkey."

Dusty lifted his head and stared at her with puffy red eyes. "He was a bad monkey?"

"Yeah, he was a bad monkey." It felt like someone else was saying the words. "He robbed the rodeo payroll."

"Really?"

"He did. He was a bad monkey. He was always spending all his money on booze and getting drunk." Linda wanted to stop the flow of the words, but she couldn't seem to hold them back. It was as though she was just a spectator. They flooded over the banks in an unstoppable torrent. "He only cared about himself. He never gave a damn about his monkey family, he never spent any time with his monkey kids, and he was a verbally abusive ass to his monkey wife. He was a real bastard."

Silence filled the cab and Linda wished she could suck back in the words. Dusty sat, looking thoughtful, taking deep breaths and snorting the snot back up his nose. His scrunched-up face was a mirror image of his father's.

"If he was that bad, it's probably a good thing he's dead then, huh?"

Linda took a couple deep breaths and gazed down at her son with unfocused eyes. "Yeah, I guess so."

Dusty nodded and pulled away from her. He wiped his nose on the back of his hand and pulled a candy from his pocket. The pair sat in the pickup and stared out at the bright lights of the arena, waiting for Dave to show up so they could go home. After a while, Linda turned on the engine so they could listen to the radio.

Riding in Taxis with
My Mother in Asia

BY TRISTAN DURST

THE FIRST TAXI RIDE WAS NOT WITH MY PHYS-
ical mother, but her voice, repeating in my mind,
telling me that I would thrive and flourish and
find myself, but also that it was perfectly acceptable to fail
and implode and move back to Mississippi and resume
living in the basement rent-free until death took me. She'd
written me a letter, tucked into my carry-on, assuring me
of all these facts. "This is going to be a good year for you.
This year is going to be a happy one. Everything is going
to be alright." I read and reread her letter on the plane,
too numb to cry.

The trip to Daegu, South Korea, took nearly thirty hours:
Columbus to Tupelo, Tupelo to Memphis, Memphis to
Houston, Houston to Seattle, Seattle to Tokyo, Tokyo to
Seoul, Seoul to Daegu. The school that hired me to teach
English to seven-year-olds for the next year wouldn't reim-
burse me for the flight until I completed six months of loyal
service. These layovers represented the cheapest way to get
from Mississippi to Korea. For fourteen-hundred dollars I
could have flown from Atlanta to Seoul in twelve hours,
but if I had fourteen-hundred dollars to burn I wouldn't
have been going overseas in the first place.

From Seattle to Seoul, I couldn't sleep: too crowded, too
lonely, too tired, too scared. After the meal, I feigned sleep,
though, to discourage the Japanese man next to me from
further conversation. Korea was the wrong country, he told
me. The people were too conservative, and the streets were

filthy. I'd be better off just walking through customs with him in Narita. I put my headphones in as I ate, but that didn't stop him from tapping me on the shoulder.

"I'm sorry, but I'm very tired," I said as the attendant took our trays away. I closed my eyes and angled my body away from him towards the window. He kept talking. After I failed to respond to three of his conversational entrées, he leaned over and placed a hand firmly on the curve of my ass. It was several seconds before I decided the light groping was too high a price to pay for silence.

The shower in my apartment didn't work. The head teacher, a petite Korean woman who never smiled, met me at the Daegu airport. Together, we took a taxi to my new home. She warned me—leaving me alone in an apartment that was nowhere near the *fully furnished* my contract had promised—that the shower was "not strong."

The next morning, I woke up two hours before I needed to be at school to make sure that I was on time and put together. I discovered that "not strong" meant "completely nonfunctional." A thin trickle of water seeped out of the showerhead, directly down the wall, without approaching the force needed to clean anything. The weak stream closely resembled the starring player in a third-grade filmstrip about the process of erosion. I decided I must be doing something wrong with the shower, and that, for the time being, I was clean and pleasant-smelling enough to meet my coworkers.

When I asked, the head teacher assured me that everything in my house was fine; I just didn't have a very powerful shower. After two days of trying everything I could think of to make the shower work, I spread a towel on the kitchen floor, heated two pots of water on the stove, and washed up as best I could in the sink.

My first day in the classroom, a Friday, I had only one student: a boy whose English name was Sonny. We sat across the table from each other with our coloring pages, and huge tears rolled down his cheeks. He kept repeating the same Korean phrase over and over. When my Korean co-teacher stuck her head in the room to check on us, I asked her what he was saying.

"He says, 'I want to go home.'"

I looked at his huge, watery eyes, and I started crying myself. "Me too, Sonny," I told him. "I want to go home, too." Despite my mother's written promises, nothing was fine.

For the three days I'd been at the school, none of my coworkers showed any interest in getting to know me, or even speaking to me. So rarely were my good mornings returned that I began to suspect I was a ghost. That Friday night, the three other foreign teachers discussed their weekend plans in the staff room as if I weren't there.

"Wanna get a drink tonight, Derrick?"

"Sure, sure. Maeve, you in?"

"Yeah, why not. Cheers."

Chris, a redheaded Canadian, looked at me and said, "See you Monday, Tristan." It was the first time any of them had spoken directly to me that day.

Home alone, I was determined to make the shower work. An hour of turning knobs and kicking the wall brought me no closer to cleanliness. I slammed my open palm against the wall of the bathroom over and over, repeating the word *fuck,* before giving up and resigning myself to another hooker bath in the kitchen sink.

By this point, it was fully dark out, and I could see my reflection in the windows over my sink. The hollow-eyed person staring back startled me. Exhausted, my face looked ashen with creeping purple streaks under my eyes. Filthy, my greasy hair matted to my head like a swimmer's cap.

Starving, my diet made entirely of the canned food and granola bars I'd packed in my luggage, since I didn't know where or how to shop. Alone, without connection, in a city of three million people, so far away from my parents and my hometown, I was already seven hours into tomorrow.

I began to sob, huge, open-mouthed gasps that shook my body. With hands that trembled in concert with my weeping, I washed my hair in the sink, burning my scalp with the water I'd heated on the stove. The pain comforted me. Away from everyone who knew me or cared to know me, I was still real.

It took another week of sink baths to persuade someone from my school to come look at my shower. The hose leading to the showerhead was clogged with silt and rust from the old pipes. The maintenance man had my shower working in ten minutes.

The next day, the head teacher cornered me. Why hadn't I told her that the shower was broken? Why didn't I ask for help? "We are here to help you," she said.

"Okay," I replied.

The phone in my apartment finally got hooked-up about five weeks into my stay in Korea. I had every intention of calling my parents and begging for a plane ticket back to America. Life overseas was too hard. Teaching was too hard. I was lonely.

So lonely, I was staying up till nearly 3:00 am every morning just to watch an American TV show where Kevin Sorbo captains a spaceship. Was this show good? Of course not. Read that sentence again: *Kevin Sorbo is a spaceship captain.* But I was so desperate to hear someone, anyone, speak English that it was a godsend to me.

Sunday morning in Korea is Saturday night in Mississippi. My father was well into his traditional Saturday twelve pack by the time the phone call went through.

Before I could get out my complaints, he said, "Shitfire, girl! I'm so proud of you, out there on your own. It's amazing."

I couldn't bring myself to contradict him. He had an image of me wandering down back alleys and living this exotic life. Was I really going to tell him that I hid in my apartment, crying and watching Kevin Sorbo, eating peanut butter sandwiches? My parents thought I was amazing. I ought to at least try to prove them right.

My mother and I first shared a taxi at the tail end of my second year in Korea. My Christmas package contained a Santa hat with black trim instead of white. I found a note tucked inside the hat. "Wear the hat when you meet me at the airport so I recognize you."

When I called home to thank my parents for my gifts and confirm the dates and times of my mother's trip, I told her, "I think you'll recognize me without the hat. There won't be that many white women at the airport."

After a short pause, she repeated, "Wear the hat." It didn't sound optional.

On December 29, I arrived at the airport a full hour before her flight was scheduled to land. I twitched and fidgeted, checking the arrivals board every twenty-seven seconds, then pulled the hat on my head the second her flight switched from EN ROUTE to ARRIVED.

Collecting her baggage and clearing customs and immigration took nearly an hour, during which I constructed ever more horrific scenarios of my mother's untimely demise in a Japanese airport bathroom. The opaque sliding glass doors, separating the no-man's land of the airport from Korea proper, opened to reveal my mother. She looked so tired and frazzled that my immediate reaction was retroactive shame about what I must've looked like two years earlier.

I began jumping in the air, waving my arms back and forth like a deranged ragdoll, shouting, "Santa hat! Santa hat! I'm wearing a Santa hat!" I ran around the arrivals barricade to hug her, and we were promptly scolded by a security guard.

Incheon International Airport is located thirty to forty minutes outside of Seoul, depending on the traffic. My mother immediately vetoed my idea that we just take the subway and insisted on getting a cab to the hotel.

In order to take a teaching job in South Korea, I acquired my passport at twenty-two. I'd had two years to grow accustomed to the reckless, high speed taxi rides. Back seats usually lacked seatbelts, and drivers seemed to believe a heavy hand with the horn substituted effectively for turn signals.

My mother acquired her passport at fifty-seven to visit me in South Korea. She had spent the past thirty years living in Mississippi's third-largest city. Population: thirty thousand. Number of taxis: zero. As our driver wove manically in and out of the post-flight rush away from the airport, my mother's fingernails dug gouges into the upholstery. "Don't let him kill us," she instructed me, more than once. Her eyes focused straight ahead. She clenched her jaw.

In Korean, I asked the driver to go a little bit slower. "My mother doesn't like it," I said.

He slowed slightly for barely two minutes, using this decrease in speed as a justification for even more honking. When we reached our first red light, he turned in the seat and told me that he'd need twice the fare we'd agreed on beforehand.

"Too expensive," I said, striking the back of his seat for emphasis. I stated our negotiated price, around forty dollars, then repeated *only, only, only,* jabbing my finger at his arm.

He held up his hands in surrender. In English he said, "Okay, okay," with a laugh.

"What was that?" my mother asked me.

"He wanted more money, but I told him no."

"All in Korean?" she asked. When I nodded, her eyes filled with tears. "I can't believe how grown up you are," she said.

When we arrived at the hotel, I tipped him ten dollars. My mother was proud of me.

Two years later, our hotel in Singapore was close enough to the subway that we only needed taxis at the end of our day when our tired legs could take us no further. The night safari at the zoo ended at 11:00 pm, right when the subway shut down for the night. During our tram ride around the zoo, we saw all the nocturnal animals, usually lying listless under rocks during the daytime. In the African Animals section, one of the elephants used its trunk to douse our electric train with water. My mother bore the brunt of it. Instead of being upset, she was delighted, as though a strict professor had singled her out for praise.

In the gift shop, she bought several elephant-themed items. An elephant-bedecked tissue holder that hadn't fit in our shopping bags prompted the taxi driver to ask my mother if elephants were her favorite animal. "They are now," she replied. "One sprayed me with water at the zoo."

"Oh, miss," the driver said in precise, British English, "that is very lucky."

"I know," she sighed in agreement.

Getting my Chinese visa required what I like to call a little bit of "light sneaking" and what my father likes to call "passport fraud." Because my Korean work visa expired in less than six months, the Chinese consulate in Seoul would not issue me a tourist visa. My mother and I had plane tickets and were set to meet in Shanghai in less than two months.

"This is the worst thing that's ever happened to me," I sobbed to her on the phone.

"Tristan," she replied, "if this is the worst thing that's ever happened to you, then you have led a truly charmed life, and you need to quit whining."

My attempts at self-pity derailed, a quick bit of internet research revealed that the law stopping me from getting my visa was entirely Korea-specific. Were I in America, I could easily obtain a visa. Were my passport in America, a visa could be placed inside it.

Further research revealed that my seven-year-old passport lacked the security microchip found in newer passports. This meant that if I hid my passport between enough papers, hypothetically, it should clear postal customs without a hitch. Once my passport was in America, my mother could forge my signature on the paperwork and send my passport to the Chinese consulate in Houston, Texas, for expedited visa service. In ten to fifteen business days, my passport would be returned to her in Mississippi, complete with tourist visa. All we had to do was change her flight to include a layover in Seoul, so I could reclaim my passport, and then we'd be off to Shanghai.

"And if you get caught," my father said when I called to explain my genius plan, "you will both go to jail."

"Pishhh," my mother said. She was listening in on the other line, and we sorted the details after my father hung up in exasperation.

Sidebar: I believe microchips were added to passports specifically so things like this couldn't happen. My new passport has a microchip, thereby cutting me off from further "light sneaking."

I believed, wholly and completely, that our hotel in Shanghai was close enough to a subway station that we wouldn't need taxis. I immediately put this theory to the test, and launched us on a quest to reach the Jade Buddha Temple as soon as we'd set our bags down in the room. The main draw for me were the two jade statues, the larger of which was nearly two meters tall, that had been imported from Burma in the 1880s. The main draw for my mother was the vegetarian restaurant run by monks on the temple grounds. We could get dinner and culture in the same spot. Everyone wins.

The Shanghai subway system is profoundly more complicated than the glossy, pull-out transit map in the *Lonely Planet* makes it appear. Our trip required two transfers, which involved going above ground and walking at least two blocks to another station. By the time we reached Changshou Road Station, we had been in overcrowded, under-ventilated subway cars for over an hour.

At the station, I didn't see a map or any signage, so I just took my best guess from the five available exits, and we started walking. After about a block, my mother said, "Honey, I'm getting very hungry."

"Sure, sure, we can eat there," I said, desperately consulting the book for any clue as to where we were.

After another block, she grabbed my arm again. "Honey," she began, but trailed off. At the exact moment she grabbed my arm, I saw the temple's hours in the guidebook. They closed at 4:00pm, and it was now 4:17pm. I turned to tell my mother this ridiculous, hilarious, not-at-all-my-fault twist of fate, only to discover that she was collapsed on the sidewalk three steps behind me, clutching her head.

Brushing away her complaints about the heat and her hunger in my determination to find this temple, I had caused my mother to drop into a dead swoon on a crowded sidewalk in a foreign country. I was the complete antithesis of filial piety. Truly, I had brought shame upon our house.

While strangers helped her to a nearby bench, I bought water and chips from the nearest 7-Eleven. We took a cab back to the hotel and ate dinner in the hotel restaurant. Each of our plates came garnished with a two-inch tall bear made entirely of salt. These bears delighted my mother, and she staged a tiny salt bear puppet show whose moral was respecting one's elders. Her delight grew into forgiveness once her belly was full.

That night, as we lay in bed, she said, "I'm not getting back on the subway."

"Of course not," I assured her.

The next morning, we agreed to pay whatever it cost for a taxi ride to the temple. The doorman at our hotel waved down a taxi. The English-speaking concierge had already written out our destination for us in Mandarin.

The ride to the temple took less than five minutes. The meter didn't change. Our fare ended up being the base charge for any cab ride, about eighty-three cents. When the taxi came to a stop, my mother turned to me, annoyance plain on her face.

"Ha ha," I said. "Who knew?"

She said nothing.

"Why don't I pay for this ride?" I asked, adding another *ha ha*.

Instead of opening the door on her side of the taxi, my mother physically crawled over me, kneeing my spleen and crushing my windpipe in the process, leaving me alone in the taxi with the door wide open.

We have not taken public transportation since. In Hong Kong, I showed the business card of a posh day spa to the taxi driver, who immediately cried, "Too close. You can walk." He motioned with his arms to shoo us out of his taxi.

"No," my mother and I whined in perfect symphonic unison. "We cannot!"

Technically, he was correct, as the day spa was located one block over from our hotel. I gave him a nice tip, and I figure he got a good story out of it. Something similar happened in Macau, only I had misread the guidebook map and was trying to take a cab *next door*.

My mother was present for my last dinner in Korea. She'd flown over to help pack up ten years of my life—to get one more stamp in her own passport. We ate dinner at my favorite restaurant with my three closest friends. Nothing about the night felt real or permanent until we were all standing on the sidewalk and I had to say goodbye. My mother flagged down the taxi, and I clung to my friends, sobbing for so long that the first taxi drove away and she had to wave down another.

This time, my mother remained calm while the speed and recklessness of the driver terrified me. "Slow down," I kept yelling through my tears. I had just said goodbye to half of the people I loved most in the world, and this idiot was going to kill me before I had the chance to say hello to the other half.

My mother took my hand and pressed it to her chest. "Just breathe," she said. "Everything is going to be alright."

She hasn't been wrong yet.

Building Wings on the Way Down

BY ADAM "BUCHO" RODENBERGER

LIAS SAT IN ONE OF THE HUNDRED CHAIRS, hard-backed with plastic seats, available in the expansive waiting room. All were empty when he arrived, all were equally uncomfortable. The walls had been painted an ice blue that made him shiver despite the warmth of the room. He sat close to the long, white half-wall that separated the waiting room from the back offices. Behind this wall sat a woman, though, had she been any shorter, he never would have known she was there. He could only see the top of her head. He watched her hair bob and move, catching the glint of her glasses every so often.

He rubbed his aching shoulders, swung his arms around as if to loosen them up, leaned back into the chair, and sighed. No one else had come in or left in the half hour he'd been here, so he wondered what the holdup could possibly be. Perhaps his appointment had been superseded by another just like him—arms aching, shoulders stiff and loose at the same time, pain rippling up the spine like a reminder of time unraveling and spooling out to spite him. Perhaps this was a more serious problem than he'd first believed (though he recognized it was serious upon waking).

He stood up, and swung each arm around in huge circles again. It seemed to help a little, but he knew he was trying to attract the woman's attention too, hoping she would slap some quick on his appointment and get him into the office faster. She either ignored him or was too short to see him move around above the white partition between them.

He sorted through the magazines on the coffee tables in each corner, as if he hadn't done so twice already. He was not shocked to find that many of them were decades out of date. It almost made sense. How many years had he spent in offices just like this one? How often had the collection of magazines in every one of those places decried the same nonsense despite the publishing dates?

Master the Perfect Swing
Take Our November Body Image Quiz
Is Your Child Out of Control?
See Our List of the Best Dressed

The sparkle of lenses in his periphery caught his attention. Doris (for this is what her nametag proclaimed, though Elias preferred to call her, simply, "the woman") had shifted positions in her chair. He could hear the rustle of papers, the soft thwack of plastic on plastic, the effervescent snap and fizz of a soda being opened. She couldn't possibly be going to lunch... could she?

Before he could finish the thought, their eyes locked. Her rheumy eyes stared out through the thick glasses, blurry behind the strong prescription. A tiny, trembling hand reached up from behind the wall and placed a sign on the countertop:

Gone to Lunch, Back in 15 Minutes.
Thank You for Your Patience.

Well then, he supposed that was that. Another fifteen minutes at least. He gave her a tiny wave and wished her a hollow bon appétit. She chewed loudly in response, never taking her eyes off him.

I bet it's because I'm of a lower order, he thought. I'm sure if I were from the Department of Virtues or the Office of Dominions, I'd be shown more respect. Right? But no, I had to end up in the Ministry of Principalities where no one is liked or respected and essentially shunned. An outsider on the inside. Fantastic.

Elias sat back down, this time against the far wall, well away from the woman's enthusiastic chewing. He reached to his left and grabbed the topmost magazine on the table, a *Popular Mechanics* from March of 1993. He flipped it open and laughed. He'd landed on an article describing a device that turned an electrical outlet into another phone line for the home or office. If only they'd known how pervasive and prevalent the cell phone was about to become a few years later. Humans were a funny lot, never lacking in entertainment value.

He had to give them credit for solar energy, though. That had been a treat to watch come to fruition. Man had essentially captured the power of the sun in tiny black panels and funneled that power into something real and tangible for use. Amazing, really, when you sat back and thought about it. Man had reached out and pulled fire from the heavens for his use on Earth, harnessed it and tried (successfully) to control it once it arrived. They were a forever surprising people, with some surprises being far more pleasant than others.

A small burp emanated from the other side of the dividing wall, followed by an "excuse me" so quiet, Elias almost missed it. He put the magazine back on the table and stretched both arms, feeling the deep ache from both shoulder blades as he did so. How to explain this pain appropriately? Was this something the doctor had seen before? Surely it was. This couldn't possibly be an anomaly. This was no case prepped and ready to be touted in medical journals as some new affliction to be battled against by men smarter than him.

A doorway opened down the hall behind the white divider. An older man with pure white hair and wearing white slacks with a matching lab coat ambled towards the woman's desk. He gave Elias a friendly smile and then looked down at a clipboard. "Elias?" he asked. "Do you prefer Elias or Mike?"

"Elias is fine," he replied, standing.

The doctor waved one hand towards the hallway, beckoning him to join. "Come on back. Let's have a look at you, see if we can't get you sorted out."

"So," the doctor began, "what's got you in a funk today? Where's the pain and what can we do to help?"

Elias absentmindedly stretched his arms again as he spoke, the ache throbbing as he spoke. "It's my shoulders. And my spine, actually. Everything in back hurts and nothing I've done seems to have helped."

"Let's get that shirt off and take a look," the doctor replied calmly. Elias removed his shirt and the doctor moved around to view his back.

"Ahh...yes. Well, it appears you've lost your wings."

"I didn't lose them. It's not like I woke up and they'd been misplaced the night before. They're not detachable... but you know this."

"I do indeed. Why do you think they've gone missing?"

"I came to you hoping you could answer that very question."

"Of course. This is more common than you might imagine. Sit up straight for a moment."

Elias did so and felt the old man's fingers tracing paths along every inch of his back, muttering his "mmhmms" and his "ohs" quietly as he measured whatever he was measuring back there. He could feel cold metal pressed against his shoulders, first the right and then the left, before the doctor began finger-prodding his way up the spine. The doctor laid both hands across each of the shoulder blades.

"Breathe deep and slow for me, please."

Elias closed his eyes, breathed in and out for a full minute as the doctor remained quiet, listening and feeling with the palms of his hands.

"Okay. Everything sounds good and seems to be in order internally. Do you feel any shortness of breath or any kind of irregular heartbeat? Any dizziness or lack of energy? Any feelings of *faithdoubt* or depression? Any nausea or sickness to speak of?"

"No... to everything," Elias replied. "Other than the absent wings and the pain across my back, I feel completely normal." The way the doctor had said the phrase made Elias smirk. Sounded like *faithedout,* which wasn't far from the same meaning, really, if one thought about it.

The doctor sat down on a stool at his desk and picked up a clipboard. The scribbling of pen strokes across the page was the only sound in the room. Black marks whispered through the air, chicken scratches made audible as Elias got dressed.

The doctor crossed his legs and laid the clipboard across his thighs. "How long have you been with the Ministry of Principalities?" he asked.

Elias stopped buttoning his shirt. How long *had* he been in the Ministry? Time moved differently on this side of eternity, both faster and slower if that were possible. Was it easier to remember his last earthly memories or to count backwards from last holy shunning to absolute first? He shrugged.

"A couple thousand years, maybe, give or take? It's hard to say, but it's been awhile."

The doctor nodded. A soft knocking came from the other side of the door.

"Enter," the doctor said, picking the clipboard back up off his lap.

The door opened a crack and a frail arm shot through holding a note. The doctor took it and unfolded it. "Thank you, Doris."

The door shut and the doctor smiled up at Elias. "It appears we have found both the problem and the solution at the same time."

Why was it always a paradox here? Elias thought. *Why couldn't there just be a straight answer to straight questions?* "Do tell," he said dryly.

"You've been chosen to return."

"Return?"

"Perhaps it's best if we walk and talk at the same time. Easier to explain if you see the process."

Elias rubbed his shoulders and rotated each arm, grimacing at the motion.

They sauntered down the long maze of hallways. Elias noticed there was no noticeable order to the way the rooms were numbered: Seven T, uno, 32Z, *IVtheta, achtundfünfzig.* "What's with the doors, doc?"

The doctor smiled. "They're constantly changing. Universal doctor humor is all. It's important to have laughter in one's daily life."

"They change? You mean the room you want moves every day?"

The doctor laughed. "Oh no. The rooms don't move, only the numbers outside move. We have everything we need in every room."

"Don't you find that kind of...I don't know, annoying?"

"That's certainly one perspective. Not one I share, but it's one of many."

They turned a corner and headed down a spiraling stairwell to the next floor. "So what's this process? Is it some kind of reattachment? How does it work?" Elias's voiced echoed noisily off the walls, seemed to travel all the way down the spiral and return up. The doctor opened the door to an adjoining hallway, held his finger to his lips, and stepped inside.

Unlike the floor of the upstairs offices, this floor appeared to be completely carpeted in thick, well-kept shag. Elias could see hundreds of doctors, nurses, and assistants all walking across the surface, but the room was completely silent; mausoleum still. The air felt different here, thicker, like an invisible buffer pressed against them to help dim any sounds. The main room was rectangular in shape and dimly lit, though if you'd asked Elias where the light was coming from, he couldn't have even guessed. Origin unknow; it was simply there and it was pleasant.

The doctor leaned in and put his hand on Elias's shoulder. "We'll need to keep our voices down here. This is where the process starts. Over on the far side of the room," he said, pointing out to his left, "we have what we call the G.O.R., or Genesis Observation Room. Come."

They walked across the carpet, a feeling Elias would later remember as walking on firm water; comfortable, but strangely unsettling as well. None of the doctors or nurses paid them any attention, not even a second look at Elias's missing wings, which he found both confusing and pleasant. They walked through the throng of people and Elias heard nothing at all, as if the whole concept of sound had been sucked out of the room leaving a vacuum of abject silence.

Elias could see (or sense?) three dedicated areas within. Each had its own walls, its own patients of specific ages within. Impossibly long glass partitions separated the rooms from the hallway. In the first, rows upon rows upon rows of swaddled infants lay; some crying, some sleeping. One, a chubby, dark-skinned child, had even figured out how to use his tiny winglets and hovered above the bed, giggling and cooing just out of reach of the workers who scrambled around quietly trying to bring him back down.

Elias had to stifle a laugh. The doctor turned and smiled, shrugged as if to say 'these things happen sometimes' before nodding over to the next room.

A second set of long glass partitions allowed Elias to see another room of immeasurable size. Clusters of teenaged children dotted the landscape as far as he could see, all sitting on the floor, each cluster surrounding an obviously older individual in a chair. A teacher of some sort, perhaps. Here a priest, there a rabbi; further on a Sikh; beyond, a Buddhist; farther out, other clusters and, he assumed, other religious leaders.

Teachers? Elias, confused, mouthed to the doctor, who only nodded and smiled as he led them both on to the third and final part of the floor. The doctor pressed his hand against a smooth part of the wall, depressing a small section. Soundlessly, a door slid open to the side of them and revealed a long hallway running alongside the impossibly long room. *Just how big was this place?*

This room, however, felt significantly different than the previous two. Where there was a pure kind of hope emanating from the glass that separated them before, something more oppressive seemed to creep through the walls here. Only adults could be seen on the other side of the glass. Elias looked more intently at the faces on the other side, many of whom simply sat at the edge of their beds in meditation while others knelt in prayer. *Like the injured from a battlefield,* Elias thought to himself.

"Exactly," said the doctor quietly.

Startled, Elias looked over.

"Oh we can speak here," he said. "Just not on the main floor. The older ones are less easily influenced by outsiders. The children tend to get more easily distracted."

"...but the outer glass in the main room...?"

"Ah. Of course. We can see them; they, however, cannot see us. Even in this hallway, we're hidden from view. An optical effect, much like the separation of the teenagers in the previous room. In there, each grouping of students and single teacher believes they are the only ones in the room; the teacher is the only person they're able to see until the message is over. In the adult's room, however, each believes their bed to be surrounded by walls, that there is privacy. And in a way, there is. None of them can see each other unless we deem it necessary. Though they can hear us through the glass if we'd like to speak to them."

Elias shook his head, feeling more confused than ever. "That sounds inhumane. It sounds...wrong. Like they're imprisoned."

The doctor stepped up to the glass and spread his arm out, motioning towards the people behind it. "You thought they seemed like the injured on a battlefield, yes?"

Elias nodded.

"That's closer to true than you might think. Some of them are younger than you; some so much older, believe it or not. As old as the very first day. We might age differently than the humans, but we still age. We may know the truth about more, but our faith is still able to be shaken to its foundation. And others have spent so much time trying to be harbingers of that truth that a paradigm shift occurs within them. They become less themselves and more human. Like they've been ripped in half and both sides are struggling to control the whole.

"These rooms are built to help them heal, to help them stitch themselves back up in whatever way they need, to give them privacy to worship in a way that returns their faith. They are working to rebuild themselves from the inside out. Some literally are soldiers coming back from a battle that's been raging for several thousands of years. So, the silence and the solitary is necessary for many in order for them to feel more like themselves."

"A hospital wing for shell-shocked believers," Elias muttered.

The doctor cocked his head and smiled. "More or less, yes."

Elias stepped back. "Wait..."

The doctor laughed. "They're all in there voluntarily. They've been given this same grand tour. They know where they are."

"So what happens when they're...better?"

The doctor cocked a thumb back over his shoulder to the impossibly large room of infants. "*And on the first day...*"

"No. We start all over?"

The doctor nodded. "Perfectly painless. You will end up being someone new, for the most part, but there is an essence, an inherent you-ness that can never been replaced. It is part of who you are no matter how much your outer appearance changes, no matter which of the faiths you're born into."

"And my wings?"

"Gone, I'm sorry to say. Not so much taken away, not like a punishment, but simply gone out of use where you're concerned. You're like a battery in need of recharging, which is what your returning will do for you."

Elias stared through the glass at nothing in particular. He could just make out the shapes of both the doctor and himself in the glare, but his eyes were unfocused as he took in all this new information. *Was this something that happened often? Would he have any of his memories left? Did he have a choice of faiths to be born into?*

"Yes; you may remember crumbs here and there in your dreams, little flashes of something familiar, but nothing substantial, I'm afraid; and no, it's a luck of the draw on that front. There are some things even we don't have control over."

"Yeah, we're gonna stop the whole reading of my mind thing, now. That's pretty unsettling while I'm working through all this."

"My apologies. As long as I've been doing this, I never fail to forget what it's like to be on the receiving end of this news for the first time. I'm endlessly fascinated and enthralled when I see it in action every day. It's quite beautiful in scope."

They stood in silence. Elias pulled on his lower lip, scratched his neck nervously. The doctor said nothing and let him mull things over. Moments later, a female nurse strolled through the room on the other side of the glass. She stopped at the bed of a man who appeared younger than Elias; clothed in medical scrubs, he sat on the edge, rubbing something between his fingers, his eyes closed and his mouth moving ever so slightly in a prayer of some sort.

She held out her hand and, without opening his eyes, the man reached out to take it. A smile lit up his face as they walked together down the aisle and out of sight.

"Where's he off to?" Elias asked.

"He's returning. Just like you'll do at some point. Some return unhealed, but we've no way of knowing who they'll turn up as, so it's been hard to discern what kind of effect that has on their personality or their psyche over time."

Elias let the statement hang between them. The doctor remained still while Elias's brain sped through question after question, finally settling on one that seemed to be the most important.

"Have I gone through this before?"

The doctor shrugged and smiled. "No idea, son. Truly, I don't know. But it makes for a real interesting question, doesn't it?"

10,000 *Things*
False Boundaries, Devastation,
and the Rebuilding of a Life
BY JACLYN MARIA FOWLER

I LIVE IN RAS AL KHAIMAH, AN OUT-OF-THE-WAY place nestled between the rolling waves of the desert sands and the salty still of the Arabian Gulf. I'm a few months into my third year here, separated by nine time zones from my family, from my friends, from my country, from another lifetime. As unsettling as starting over is, I have begun to feel comfortable here. But isn't that the way it goes? We feel out of place. We learn to survive. We adapt. We regain our equilibrium. We begin to live again.

While I call Ras al Khaimah home, it certainly isn't Home. Home—with a capital H—is still firmly planted among the mountains of northeastern Pennsylvania. It is where my mom's heart—older and weaker—still beats, still calls to me. But now I live in the Middle East, an almost new person. I travel more. I spend more time in cities as opposed to the small towns of my old life. I eat different foods, dabble in yoga, meditate, and forgo alcohol. I do not wear a headscarf, but I have learned to respect the women who choose to wear one. I speak Arabic...poorly, haltingly... but even this is changing.

This morning as I prepare for work, I wonder for the zillionth time, *how did I end up here?* Like a PowerPoint presentation on loop, I see images, I hear voices, I re-experience scenes of my past. I dream about home in my sleep. And in my waking hours. There are times when I swear I hear my dad's voice, my mom's laugh, or feel the phantom chill of the season's first nor'easter. Like the ghost pains that plague those who have lost limbs, my pains are those of a lost life. *How did I end up here?*

On my way to Dubai now, I switch on the NPR podcast, already nine hours stale, but still the most current, most trustworthy news I can get. It is always the same these days: Trump, Trump and the sex tape, the hurricane, Syria, Trump, Trump and the Russians. *Dear God,* I pray, I scream, I plead, *let it end, this hateful election.* Let it end. I have not yet figured out why I am so deeply affected by it all. In time, I will make the connection. This new mind-track crashes into the loop of the one already playing, ceaselessly searching for an answer to the question, *how did I end up here?* While the Trump-track does not interfere with the original thought-track, it does give me something new to consider when the two meet in my mind. *I'm here so I don't have to deal directly with Trump,* I think. Then just as quickly, the silent arbiter of my revelations—track number three, if you're keeping count—chimes in, *nope, that's not it.*

Look at me, the sun insists, just beginning its ascent. Here, when the sun calls, desert dwellers take heed; its powerful, deadly heat rules the desert. Yet, as with all things, there is balance. The sunrise here is magnificent, breathtaking. In its almost-equator enormity, the sun sizzles, its ray-hands gyrating in the early morning air; the desert floor shimmers and dances in response. Track four—the sunrise—has been initiated, providing yet more competition for all the other disparate thoughts taking up space in my mind.

"On May 31, 2015, Austin Beggin's life changed forever," the disembodied voice reports from the car radio; it interrupts my thoughts, interrupts the sunrise. "I know what that's like," I say out loud to no one. As I turn onto the highway, the final moments of the sun's passage from desert floor to sky moves behind me and out of view. So with words and phrases I almost hear—*wave, face down, paralyzed from the neck*—my scattered focus begins a shift to NPR.

But before the shift is complete, something new intrudes, catching my eye. Off to one side of the highway, a truck in the right-hand lane. Like a stubby little arm turned up at the elbow in muscle pose, the truck's side mirror holds a compressed version of the sunrise taking place behind us, miniature explosions of orange and gold in a confined space. "Maybe this is why I'm here," I whisper. And it seems as good a reason as any. To see the sun's majesty manifested and magnified in a mirror the size of a forearm seems to answer the question that relentlessly, achingly runs through my mind, *how did I end up here?* I do not fully grasp its meaning yet, but I have a sense that I will. With time. The driver of the truck notices me staring. I nod and smile. He pushes hard on the accelerator.

"In every sort of lifetime, we can do about 10,000 things," a radio voice calls me back inside the little red Nissan. A therapist is giving advice to the newly paralyzed character at the heart of the NPR story—Austin Beggin. "So, what's gonna happen now," the therapist says, "is you're going to do a different 10,000 things than you were gonna do before." And just like that, all the thought-tracks in my mind come to a full stop, a screeching of brakes on the road of my mind. For the first time since rolling out of bed this morning, I am fully engaged in one thing: the 10,000 things. *This, this, the silent arbiter of my mind urges, this is why you're here.*

In January 2013, I was fired from a job by a man, an army-officer-turned-pseudo-educator with an abundance of autocratic-like qualities. In one fell swoop, I had been expelled from my profession, my passion, my life, from the way I perceived myself, from the way others perceived me. I had been abused and mistreated by a man—an ex-lieutenant colonel who threw his physique; his deep, overpowering voice; and his ugly views of the world into the faces of all those who stood in opposition to him, silent or otherwise. An oppressive bully, a demagogue, he fought against anything or anyone—especially a woman—who threatened his view of himself as "the fucking president" of a little private school. We—the two of us—represented a paradox of epic proportions; I would be the one to pay for it.

He peddled half-truths and deceptions, smears and conspiracies until he believed them himself. And through the conviction of his own beliefs, others began to believe them as well. Even when they did not. Too often, I disrupted his authoritarian tendencies. Too often, I spoke the truth when others feared to. "Please say something," they would beg me before meetings, and I would. Always politely, of course. Always professionally. Much too often, however, my words threatened his view of how women should behave. Deferentially, mostly. Especially when it came to him. And when he finally recognized my honest resistance to the fear he sowed, he shut me down—just a woman, he believed—with all the vengeance and fury he could muster.

Mine is not an isolated story. Rather, many many people have seen their lives destroyed, their worth diminished, because they have been viewed through the lens of a single characteristic: woman, black, refugee, Muslim, gay. I am a woman. One man used my woman-ness to dismiss my abilities, my thoughts, my worth. His peculiar combination of authoritarianism and misogynistic tendencies could only see part of me—the woman part—and the rest of me conflicted with his views on what Woman *should* be. The consequence to me, of course, was that he was able to strip me of the full range of who I am to create a simple, definable boundary. This boundary gave him a way to ratchet up his ugly rhetoric and corresponding behaviors, granting him access to a righteous indignation, a sense of being the victim, a designation which he did not deserve. In turn, I became the "other," the hated, the despised, and eventually the hunted. While most could see this evolving, many feared retribution for speaking out against it. My life was devastated, at least initially, and changed irrevocably as a result. A few years later, I left home for the Middle East because I had to. Because I needed a job to care for my children. I took my first step to reconstituting my 10,000 things. My different 10,000 things.

After only four months in the United Arab Emirates, I took my second step. I married. A Muslim. A Palestinian. A refugee. All in one man. Although he was born and raised in Lebanon, my husband is a citizen of nowhere, a man without a home country. Like the wind, he has no real point of origin; there is no place for him to die. His parents arrived in Lebanon as toddlers after being safely transported from their homes in Haifa during the Arab-Israeli War of 1947. Their families were assured they would be allowed to return when the fighting subsided. "Only a few weeks," they were told, so the families locked the doors of their homes, left everything behind—furniture, family photos, money, memories, neighbors, everything—and traveled temporarily to Lebanon. A forced vacation of sorts, fully expecting to return home. They are still waiting. For 68 years, they have lived as refugees, bearing sons and daughters, grandchildren, and great-grandchildren without any hope of citizenship. Most of the world, I have learned, is neither gracious nor fair-minded when it comes to some singular characteristics: Muslim, Palestinian, refugee, among them.

Fadi and I met at work and became friends, best friends. He challenged me on topics of religion and ethics.

I challenged him on his rigid views about the West, views mostly derived from movies. One night, as he helped my son put a new bike together, he acted distracted, edgy.

"What's wrong with you?" I asked.

He looked down, not at me, and mumbled, "Will you marry me?"

I gagged. Not a good first response to a marriage proposal. But he had surprised me, had caught me completely off-guard. To me, a date or two had always seemed a reasonable expectation as a precursor to marriage. But Fadi didn't date. Muslim men do not date, he told me.

"No. Don't," he tried to discourage the gag reflex in me. "I promise you'll love me."

Fadi spent the next few minutes laying out his case. He then spent the next few days awkwardly asking me to consider his offer before accepting or rejecting it. "Just think about it, okay?" A few weeks later, I consented.

"Dad?" I asked over Skype, "This is Fadi."

"What's his name?" my dad asked, acting as if only I could hear him.

"Fadi."

"Family? His name is Family?"

"Fadi," I corrected, flushing.

"What the hell kind of name is Family?" my dad asked.

"FADI," I shouted through the screen at him. "F-A-D-I."

Somehow my dad had intuited something big was coming, and he wasn't going to make it easy.

"Fadi? Well what the hell kind of name is Fadi?"

My mother waved a tiny wave at the computer screen. "Hi, Jaclyn," she chirped. Rapidly declining under the curse of Alzheimer's, my mother no longer had any pretense, nor had she any remaining scripts for communicating competently. Smiling blankly had mostly taken the place of engaging. "Are you still American?" she asked.

"I am, Mom. Don't worry." She waved her tiny wave again.

"Hello, Jack," Fadi interrupted.

My dad raised his eyebrows. This man—sitting thousands of miles away with his youngest daughter—was already calling him by his first name.

"You don't know me," Fadi started.

"Damn right," my father interrupted.

"But I want you to trust me."

"Why the hell would I trust you?"

This has started off well, I thought.

Fadi pushed on, explaining how we had met. We had become friends, something that, Fadi tried to explain, was unusual in this part of the world. Men. Women. Blah. Blah. Blah. He talked about his own family and said that he wanted to honor me by making me happy. After several minutes, Fadi paused to assess my father's mood.

"I can't understand a word he's saying."

"Dad," I said embarrassed, "he can hear you."

"Well, I can't understand him," he said again to me, not to Fadi.

Fadi, still in high spirits, started again. He spoke slower, pausing from time to time to allow my father to catch up. And then he asked.

"May I have your permission to marry your daughter?"

It was the first thing my father had understood all night.

"I don't know you," my dad shouted at Fadi's request.

"Dad!" I whined at the screen, "Be nice."

"I like him," my mom offered blankly, finally noticing Fadi. "I think he's handsome."

"Jesus, Joanne, you don't even know him."

She smiled, undeterred by my father's words, and waved a tiny wave at me. "Hi, Jaclyn."

"Hi, Mom."

Fadi tried again. He listed all the reasons why he would

be a good husband. He talked about his plans for the future. He smiled broadly, believably, and gestured at my father.

"So would you give me your blessing, Jack?" Fadi asked.

"My blessing?" he asked in a way that said *no.*

"I like him. He's handsome," my mom said again.

"Jesus, Joanne, shut up."

She smiled. And waved. "Hi, Jaclyn."

"Hi, Mom."

We were in full blown Fowler mayhem, going nowhere. Based on the experiences of my past, I knew we would continue to go nowhere fast. But Fadi, who was not at all flustered, spoke again.

"Jack, I love her."

I stopped. Turned to Fadi. Teared up. I hadn't heard him say it before. I hadn't heard anyone say it for a very long time. My dad noticed and stopped talking. After a few minutes, my father, calmer now, resumed.

"You love her?"

"I do." And turning to me, Fadi said, "Tell him I don't lie." And turning to my father, he said, "I don't lie."

My father's eyes welled up. He looked at my mom who continued to look blankly at the computer screen in front of her. From time to time, she waved, and I waved back. But my dad? I knew what he was thinking. With Fadi's declaration of love, my father considered the woman sitting next to him—my mom—and their long life together. I could see the pain of my mother's Alzheimer's in my father's eyes. I understood how his heart broke for the love that was still between them—would always be between them—but because of my mother's illness, it could not be expressed. My mother sat smiling, unaware, in the same way she had since the beginning of the conversation, but Fadi's declaration had softened my father.

"Do you love him?" my father asked.

"I don't know," I responded.

This was not the answer he expected.

"You're both nuts." My father threw up his hands in exasperation. "Do what you want. You're old enough."

Fadi looked confused.

"He said yes," I told him. "Kind of."

"Yes?" Fadi asked my dad.

"It's up to her. She's old enough."

"I like him. He's handsome," my mom said again.

"You better like him. He's going to marry her," my dad said.

"Who's getting married?" my mom asked.

"For God's sake, Joanne. Jaclyn. Jaclyn's getting married."

"To who?" she asked innocently.

"To Fadi, Mom," I answered.

When she turned to look at me, I pointed at Fadi.

"Oh, good. He's handsome," she replied.

"I'm Muslim," Fadi announced nervously. "And Palestinian."

"I'm happy for you," my dad responded, screwing up his eyes. He did not understand the relevance of Fadi's revelations.

Then Fadi spoke again, "Can I call you Dad?"

"He couldn't stop while he was ahead, could he?" my dad asked me, rolling his eyes and shaking his head.

I married Fadi on a Friday in December at the home of a Jordanian judge. I wore a scarf. I had to. The court system in the UAE is Islamic; as such, everyone must follow the traditional rules.

"But it's not *my* belief," I sulked. Fadi tenderly drew the scarf around my head.

"I'm so happy," he announced, ignoring my pout.

"All the wedding pictures with this?" I gestured to the scarf.

Fadi's hands trembled as he made the final loop of scarf around my neck.

"You wear veils in the West," he proposed as a way to settle me. I balked.

An hour after arriving as a single woman in hijab, I left the judge's home as a wife. I smiled and held Fadi's hand for the first time. Then I remembered my earlier distress, tore the scarf off my head, and cut up all the pictures of me in hijab. Fadi kept one; it is still in his wallet.

One year after marrying, we decided to begin the process of returning to America. Together. I saw this as another of the 10,000 things of my new life. We hired a Washington lawyer. We filled out paper after paper after paper, paying progressively higher and higher fees. I volunteered at the American Consulate in Dubai, hoping to better understand the immigration process. Things were proceeding beautifully. Then, at a critical juncture, Trump burst onto the American political scene, called for a ban on Muslims, and quelled our enthusiastic march towards returning to America. I now find myself in the odd situation of having had one hate-filled misogynistic man push me from my home country and another hate-filled misogynistic man who has the potential of keeping me from returning, all because both have chosen to define multi-nuanced individuals through the lens of just one characteristic.

I am a woman, but who I am encompasses so much more than that. Likewise, Fadi is a Muslim man, a Palestinian, a refugee. But this is too limited a definition of him. He is a brilliant math teacher, one of the best I've ever seen. Despite the odds, he is well educated, even now pursuing a master's degree. He is a father of three, kind and generous and attentive to his children, hardly ever missing a single dinner with them. He is a stepfather to two, using humor to guide my children, using love to bond them to him. He is a son, a brother, a friend, the e-Learning Coordinator at his school. He is a mentor, a practical joker, a man who was a nationally rated table tennis player and rated again in chess. He is a musician and the worst handyman I have ever met. He is the love of my life, my husband. And I am his wife. A woman. And so much more.

How did I end up here? I came to understand that the actions of others frequently hurt, but our own reactions modulate the power differential in the interaction. I ended up here, then, to choose to hold on to my power in the face of a life devastated by one man's narrow definition of the multi-faceted, many-sided me. *So, how did I end up here?* I have come to take a stand against a boundary that forced me into the role of "other," and I have come as witness in support of the other "others." *How did I end up here?* I am here to understand that the sun's majesty manifested and magnified in a mirror the size of a forearm is a visceral reminder of the potential of self-regeneration. In other words, I have come to live out my new 10,000 things.

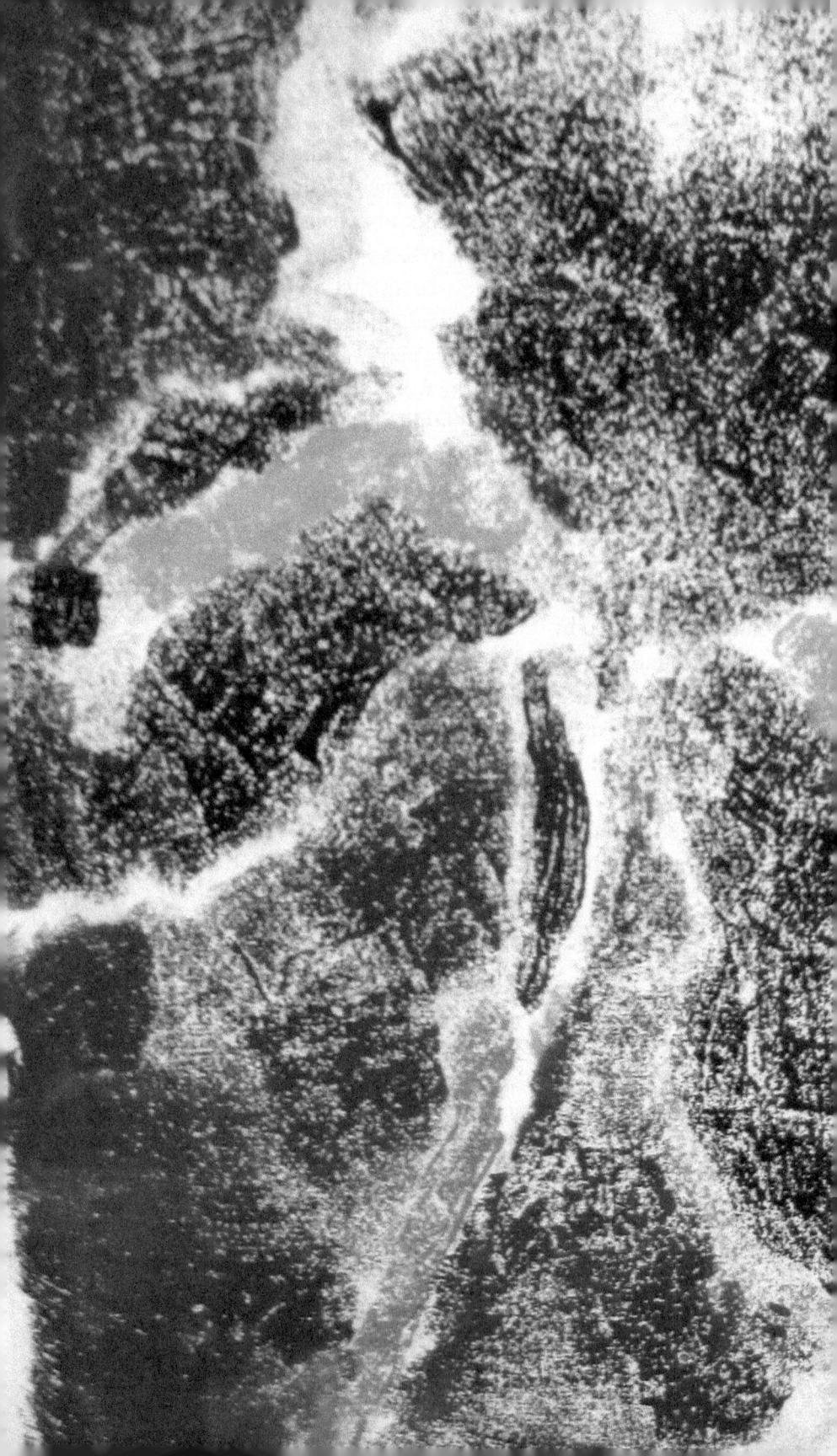

IRIS; AFTER AYERS; MAGENTA AND YELLOW 1   2011

biographies

Sherman Chaddlesone Flash Fiction Contest

WINNER

BART EVERSON

Bart Everson is a writer, a baker of bread, a husband and a father. An award-winning videographer, he is co-creator of ROX, the first TV show on the internet. After being run out of Indiana on a rail, he helped found the Green Party of Louisiana as well as Friends of Lafitte Greenway, a nonprofit that has played a key role in constructing a greenway through the heart of New Orleans.

FINALISTS

MATTIE LEE ELLIOTT

Mattie Lee Elliott is a former English major and current office worker living in Oklahoma City. She believes in the power of words to make sense of the world.

ROSS WHITE

Ross White was born and raised in Edmond, and has a fondness for things fantastical and magical.

MEGAN THOMSON CONNOR

Megan Thomson Connor is based in New York where she lives with her dog George. She minored in creative writing as an undergraduate student at Bryn Mawr College. She was last published in Sarah Lawrence's Lumina.

JOSH SHEPARD

Josh Shepard is a writer, filmmaker, and serial collector. He holds a Bachelor of Arts in Creative Writing from the University of Central Oklahoma. He resides in Oklahoma City with his girlfriend and his cat.

JULIE GARCÉS

Julie Garcés was born and raised Miami, FL and now lives in Los Angeles. Her work has been analyzed and workshopped in bohemian writing circles, has appeared in tattered backpacks and been stuck in office copy machines. Her biggest fan/muse is her special needs cat, who sits on her lap while she types.

KALYN MCALISTER

Kalyn McAlister graduated from Oklahoma State University with a Bachelors in Human Development and Psychology. Currently she is in the Creative Writing MA program and writes poetry, short story, and long fiction. Her academic focus is rhetoric and composition, which she teaches freshman. McAlister's work, both academic and creative, attempts to bend genre by playing with form and combining elements across disciplines.

Poetry

TOBI COGSWELL ALFIER

BLUEHORSEPRESS.COM

Tobi Cogswell Alfier is a multiple Pushcart nominee and a Best of the Net nominee. Her current chapbooks include *Down Anstruther Way (Scotland Poems)* from FutureCycle Press, and her full-length collection *Somewhere, Anywhere, Doesn't Matter Where* is forthcoming from Kelsay Books. She is co-editor of *San Pedro River Review.*

C. WADE BENTLEY

WADEBENTLEY.WEEBLY.COM

C. Wade Bentley lives, teaches, and writes in Salt Lake City. His poems have appeared in many journals, including *Best New Poets, Rattle, Cimarron Review, Poetry Northwest,* and *Pembroke Magazine.* A full-length collection, *What Is Mine,* was published by Aldrich Press in January of 2015. Further information about his publications and awards can be found at wadebentley.weebly.com.

STUART JAMES FORREST
STUARTFORREST@ATT.NET
Stuart James Forrest, born in Omaha, Nebraska in 1951, is now a retired public servant living in Foster City, California. He developed a passion for creative writing while attending Stanford University. He enjoys writing poetry and short stories, and hopes to develop enough skill to be a strong, creative representative of his generation of Black Americans who lived through a very tumultuous period in American history. He takes his inspiration from his faith and a desire to reflect his spiritual struggles in everything he writes.

PETER HOGAN
Peter Hogan is a third year MFA candidate in Poetry at the University of Memphis. He is a past Poetry Editor and Senior Poetry Editor at *The Pinch Literary Journal*. He is the recipient of the 2016 Deborah Talbot Award sponsored by The Academy of American Poets. He has recent publications in *Yemassee* and *Mulberry Fork Review*.

DAVID MIHALYOV
David Mihalyov lives outside of Rochester, NY, with his wife, two daughters, and two dogs. His poems have appeared in several journals, including in *Concho River Review, Gravel,* and *Timberline Review*.

JEANETTA CALHOUN MISH
Jeanetta Calhoun Mish is the 2017-2018 Poet Laureate of Oklahoma Her most recent collection is *What I Learned from the War* (West End, 2016). She is the Director of the Red Dirt MFA Program at Oklahoma City University, and, since 2007, has edited Mongrel Empire Press, a CLMP small press dedicated to regional and unusual literary works.

NATE PRITTS

NATEPRITTS.COM

Nate Pritts is the Director and Founding Editor of H_NGM_N (2001), an independent publishing house that started as a mimeograph 'zine, and the author of eight books of poetry, including *Decoherence,* which won the 42 Miles Press Poetry Award and will be published in the fall of 2017. He lives in the Finger Lakes region of NY State.

TIM ROLANDS

Tim Rolands is a software engineer, type designer, digital artist, and writer. His poems have been published in *Paintbrush: A Journal of Poetry and Translation* as well as *The New Press Literary Quarterly.* He has served as poetry editor at Truman State University Press and edited *Cat's Ear Poetry & Fiction* (1992-94). Originally from St. Louis, he now lives in central Wisconsin with his wife and daughter.

PETER SERCHUK

PETERSERCHUK.COM

Peter Serchuk's poems have appeared in a wide variety of journals in the US and UK including *Antiphon, Allegro, Boulevard, Poetry, Denver Quarterly, New Letters, Texas Review, American Poetry Review, North American Review, Atlanta Review* and others. His work has also appeared on *Garrison Keillor's The Writer's Almanac* as well as in more than a half-dozen anthologies. His collections include *Waiting for Poppa at the Smithtown Diner* (University of Illinois Press) and *All That Remains* (WordTech Editions).

KAREN J. WEYANT

Karen J. Weyant's poetry prose has been published in *Cold Mountain Review, Copper Nickel, Harpur Palate, Poetry East, Rattle, River Styx,* and *Whiskey Island.* She is the author of two poetry chapbooks, *Stealing Dust* (Finishing Line Press, 2009) and *Wearing Heels in the Rust Belt* (winner of Main Street Rag's 2011 chapbook contest). She teaches at Jamestown Community College in Jamestown, New York. When she is not teaching, she explores the rural Rust Belt of northern Pennsylvania and western New York.

Graphic Shorts

JASON HART

SHOWERSTORM.TUMBLR.COM

Jason Hart is a writer, comics cartoonist, and marketing designer based in Ohio. He graduated from The Art Institute of Pittsburgh in 2005 and works as an Art Director for a Dayton ad agency. In the off hours, he is a father. In the wee hours, he makes funny books. His most recent stories have been featured in Ink Brick, fēlan, and Gigantic Sequins. Jason is also a founding member of the Dayton Comics Club, an open group which meets weekly to talk about and create comics.

JASPER SCHELLEKENS-CARRÉ

Jasper Schellekens-Carré is part of the School of Bitches comics collective. Once upon a time he won 3rd place for an essay on the importance of algebra. He hasn't used algebra since.

Visual Art

HOLLY DAY

Holly Day's published books include the nonfiction books *Music Theory for Dummies, Music Composition for Dummies, Guitar All-in-One for Dummies, and Piano All-in-One for Dummies.* Her poetry books are *Ugly Girl* (Shoemusic Press) and *The Smell of Snow* (ELJ Publications). Her needlepoints and beadwork have recently appeared on the covers of *Your Impossible Voice, Sinister Wisdom,* and *QWERTY Magazine.*

JOHN TIMOTHY ROBINSON

John Timothy Robinson is a graduate of the Marshall University Creative Writing program. John is also a twelve-year educator in Mason County, WV. He is a published poet with work appearing in twenty-nine literary journals and websites since August 2016. In Printmaking, his primary medium is Monotype and Monoprint process with interest in collagraph, lithography, etching and nature prints.

JURY S. JUDGE

Jury S. Judge is an artist, writer, poet, and political cartoonist. She is a contributor to *The Noise,* a literary arts and news magazine serving Northern Arizona. Her *Astronomy Comedy* cartoons are also published in *The Lowell Observer.* Her artwork and photography will be published in the upcoming issues of *THAT Literary Review, Dodging The Rain,* and *Duende.* She has been interviewed on *NAZ Today* for her work as a political cartoonist. She graduated Magna Cum Laude with a BFA from the University of Houston-Clear Lake in 2014.

ANNA MARTIN

WWW.VACANTIA.ORG

Anna Martin is a digital/traditional artist, writer and photographer based out of Saint Augustine, Florida. She is an avid explorer and much of her artwork is inspired by her travels and life experiences, and she strives to capture emotions and inspire others with her work. Her work has been previously exhibited in various galleries and museums, such as the Rosenberg Gallery and the Baltimore Museum of Art, and has also been published in various art magazines such as *Grub Street* and *Plenilune Magazine.* Anna is a freelance artist, and is always looking for new work and collaborative projects. Anna also frequently works under the pseudonym Vacantia, and more of her art can be found at her online gallery.

ALYSSA WILLIAMS

Alyssa Williams is a photographer who strives to break away from the conventional. She became interested photography at a young age and continues to follow her passion. Williams loves sharing her work with those who are interested.

CHRISTOPHER WOODS

CHRISTOPHERWOODS.ZENFOLIO.COM

Christopher Woods is a writer, teacher and photographer who lives in Chappell Hill, Texas. His published works include a novel, *The Dream Patch,* a prose collection, *Under a Riverbed Sky,* and a book of stage monologues for actors, *Heart Speak.* HIs short fiction has appeared in many journals including *The Southern Review, New Orleans Review,* and *Glimmer Train.* He conducts private creative writing workshops in Houston.

Plays

TERESA MIRLL

Teresa Mirll is a graduate student completing a second Masters in English Literature at the University of Central Oklahoma. In 2014, she completed her Masters of Fine Arts thesis, a collection of short stories called *The Pop-Up Principle.* Teresa won the 2013 Geoffrey Bocca Outstanding Graduate Student in Creative Writing Award for her short fiction. She lives in Edmond, Oklahoma.

Prose

SHAWN CAMPBELL

Shawn Campbell was born in Eastern Oregon. He currently resides in Portland where he works as an economist and lives with a house plant named Morton. He has had numerous short stories published, and his first book, *The Uncanny Valley,* is available for purchase on Amazon, Barnes and Noble, and Kobo.

LESLIE DAVIS

Leslie Davis completed her BFA at the Rhode Island School of Design, and studied writing at Brown University. Kevin McIlvoy has since been her mentor. She currently resides in South Florida with her husband.

TRISTAN DURST

Tristan Durst is a recent graduate of the MFA program at Butler University, where she served as the fiction editor for *Booth*. She once ate so many Sweet Tarts the inside of her mouth began bleeding.

JACLYN MARIA FOWLER

Jaclyn Maria Fowler earned a doctorate in education from Penn State and an MFA in creative writing from Wilkes University. She is an adventurer, a lover of culture and language and people in general. Fowler is an American woman of Irish descent married to a Palestinian man who works as an associate professor at Canadian University in the United Arab Emirates.

KELLY GROGAN

Kelly Grogan is an emerging writer from Santa Barbara, California. She received my MFA from Antioch University, Los Angeles. Her work is forthcoming in *The Tishman Review,* and was shortlisted for the Iowa Review Fiction Award.

ADAM "BUCHO" RODENBERGER

Adam "Bucho" Rodenberger is a surrealist writer from Kansas City. He released his first short story collection, *Scaring the Stars into Submission,* in 2016 and is set to release his second collection, *The Machinery of the Heart: Love Stories* in 2018, and a third collection, *Under the Black Rainbow,* in 2019.

SUBMISSION INFORMATION

New Plains Review accepts original work in poetry, prose, and visual art. Submission information and editorial guidelines are accessible through the website.

ORDERING INFORMATION

Pricing for current and back issues are available through Amazon.

COLOPHON

Huronia was designed by Ross Mills, co-founder of Tiro Typeworks. *Skolar Sans* was designed by David Březina and Sláva Jevčinová. *Huronia* and *Skolar Sans* are released through the Rosetta Type Foundry.

www.ingramcontent.com/pod-product-compliance
Lightning Source LLC
Chambersburg PA
CBHW051516170626
46811CB00002B/854